My Mazes 1 - Medium

My Mazes 2 - Simple

My Mazes 3 - Simple

My Mazes 4 - Simple

My Mazes 5 - Medium

My Mazes 6 - Medium

My Mazes 7 - Simple

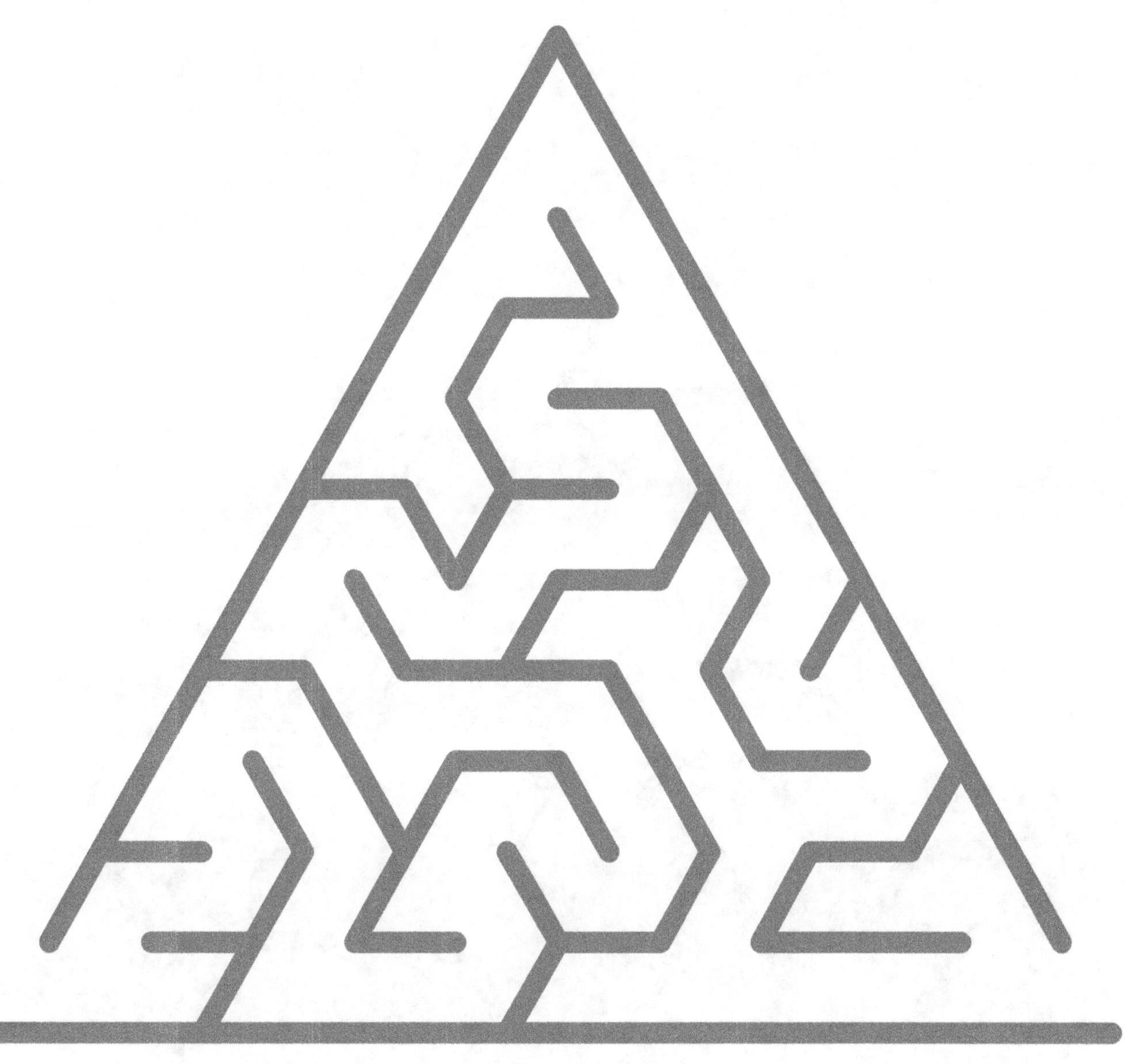

My Mazes 8 - Simple

My Mazes 9 - Simple

My Mazes 10 - Medium

My Mazes 11 - Medium

My Mazes 12 - Medium

My Mazes 13 - Medium

My Mazes 14 - Medium

My Mazes 15 - Medium

My Mazes 16 - Medium

My Mazes 17 - Simple

My Mazes 18 - Medium

My Mazes 19 - Medium

My Mazes 20 - Medium

My Mazes 21 - Medium

My Mazes 22 - Simple

My Mazes 23 - Medium

My Mazes 24 - Simple

My Mazes 25 - Simple

My Mazes 26 - Simple

My Mazes 27 - Simple

My Mazes 28 - Simple

My Mazes 29 - Simple

My Mazes 30 - Medium

My Mazes 31 - Simple

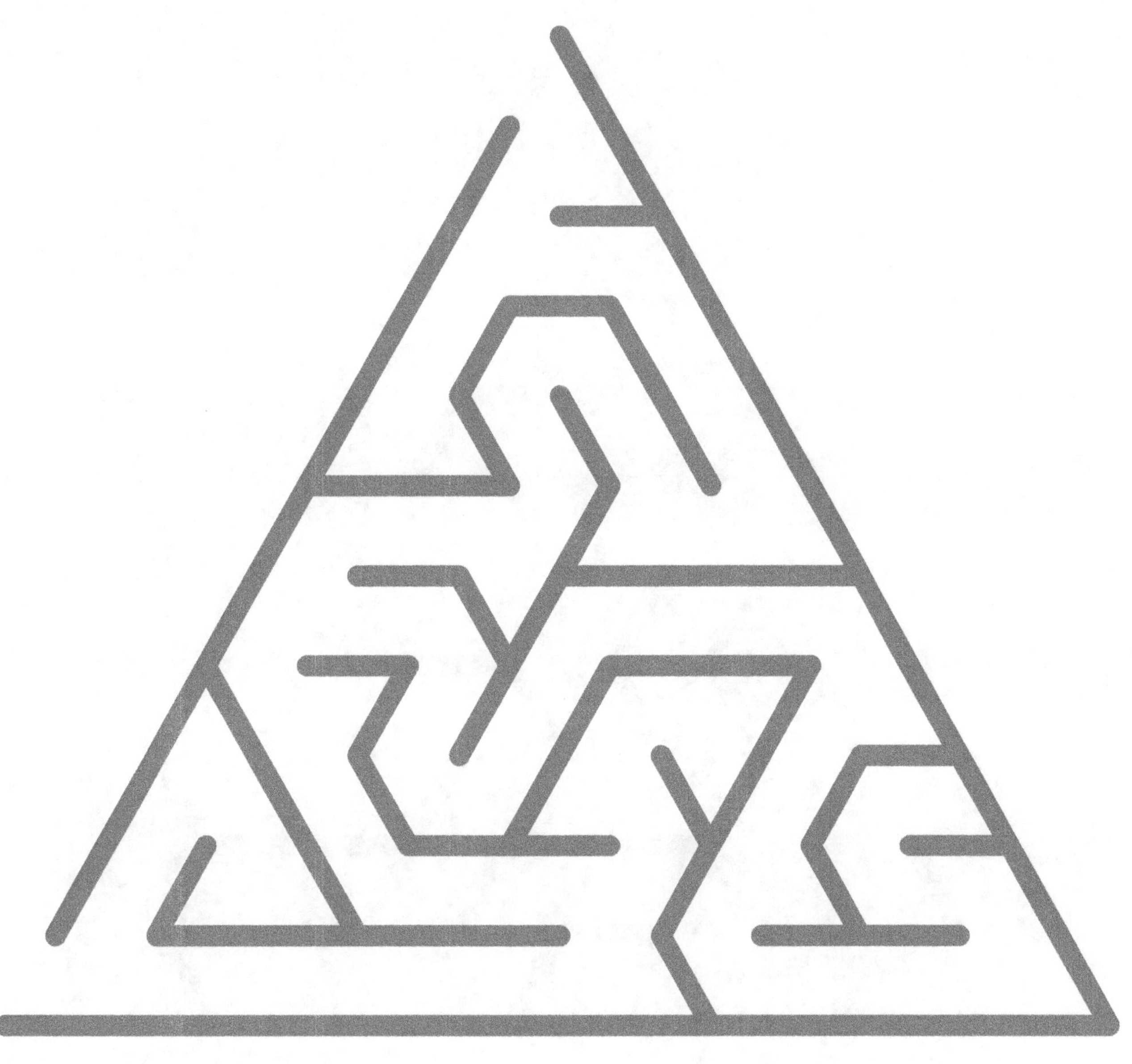

My Mazes 32 - Simple

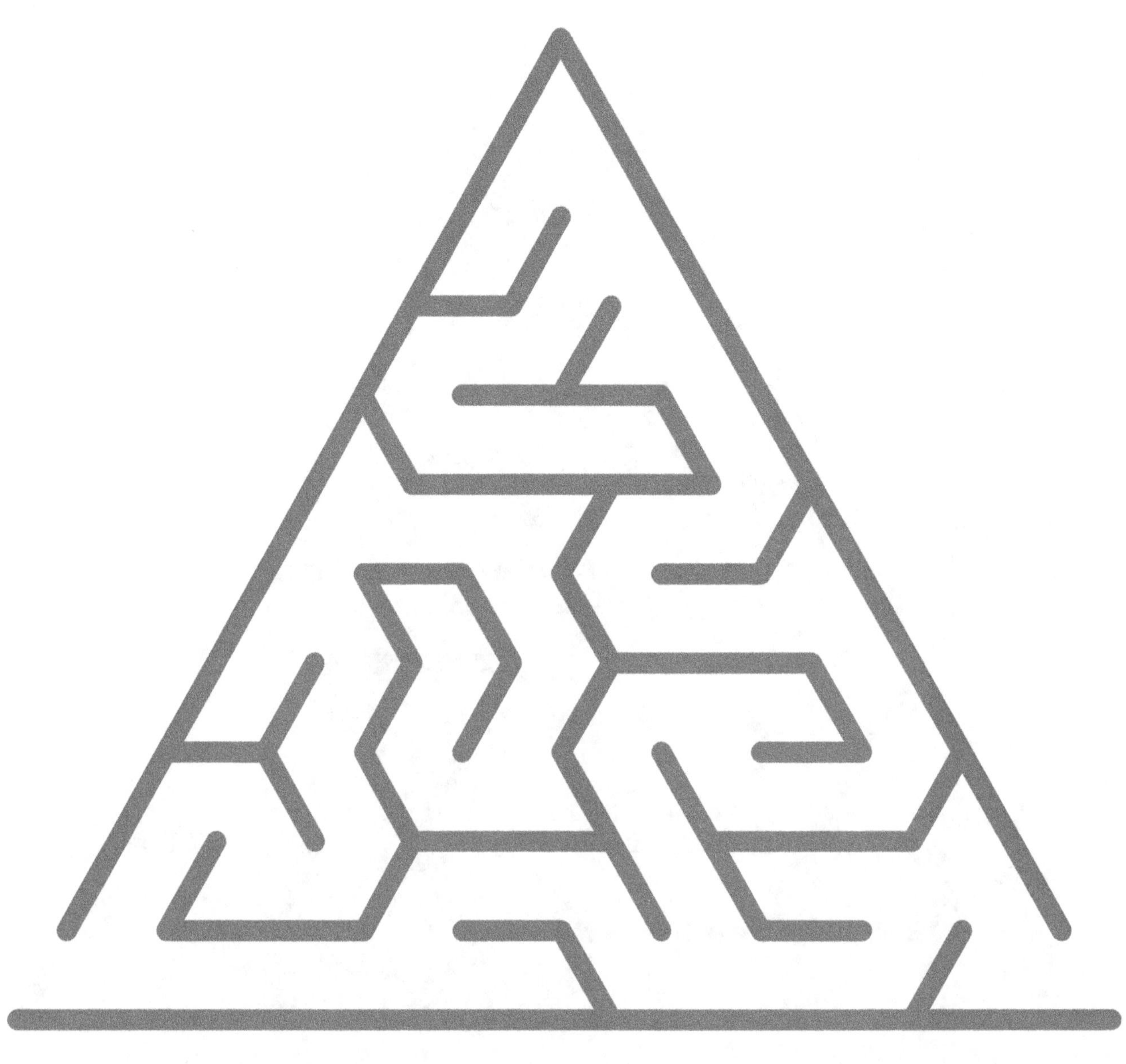

My Mazes 33 - Medium

My Mazes 34 - Medium

My Mazes 35 - Simple

My Mazes 36 - Medium

My Mazes 37 - Simple

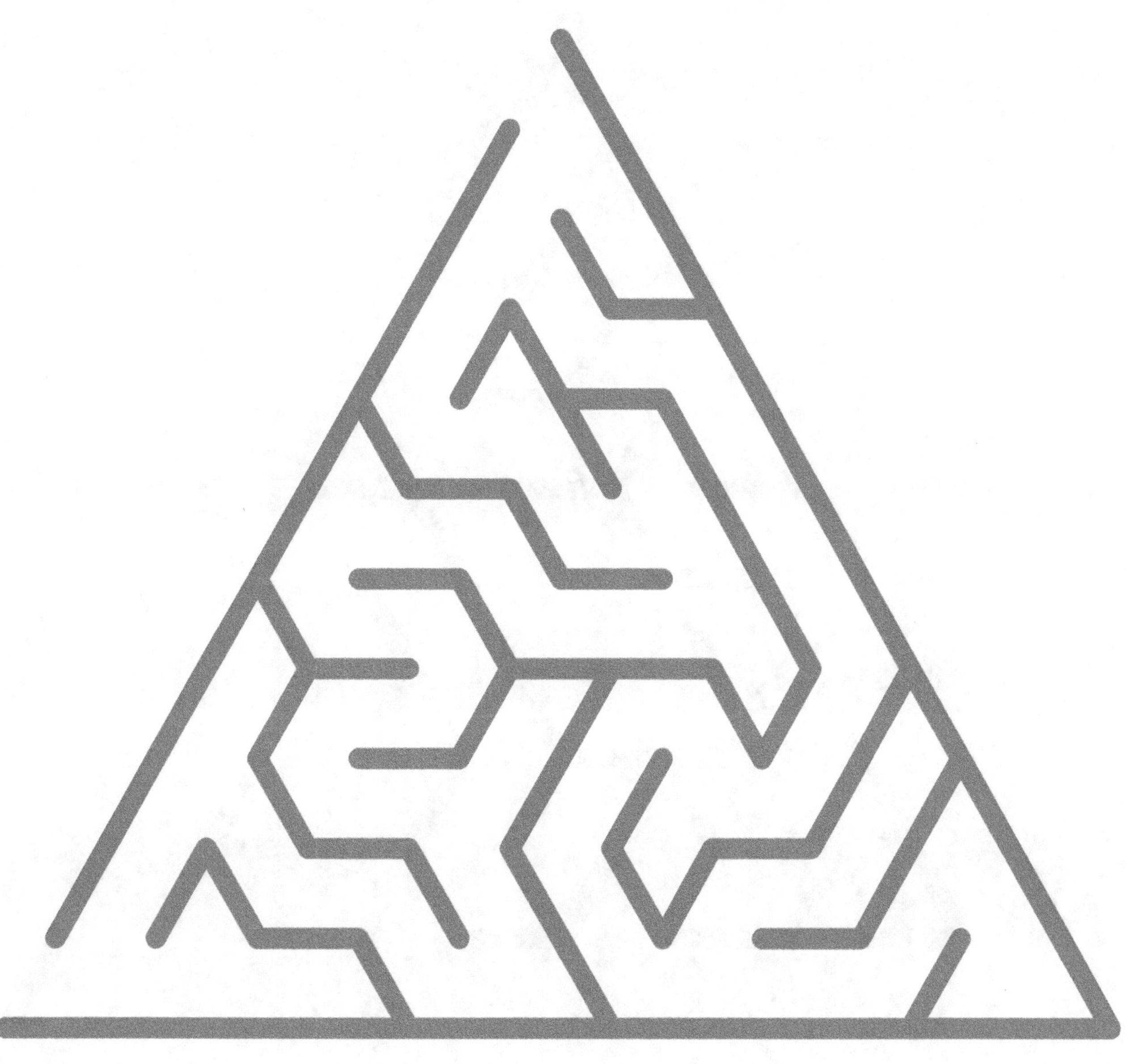

My Mazes 38 - Simple

My Mazes 39 - Simple

My Mazes 40 - Simple

My Mazes 41 - Simple

My Mazes 42 - Medium

My Mazes 43 - Medium

My Mazes 44 - Simple

My Mazes 45 - Simple

My Mazes 46 - Simple

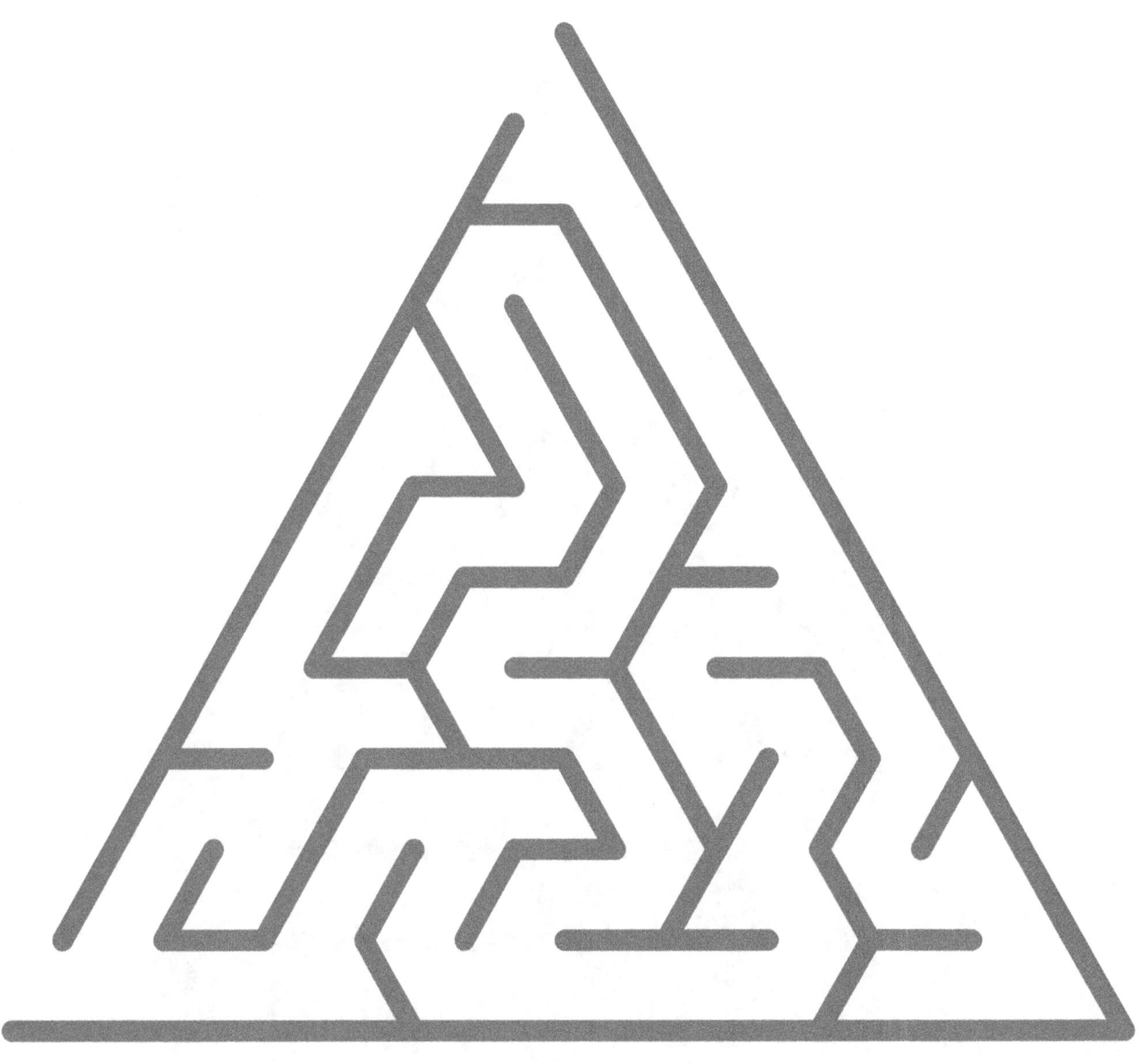

My Mazes 47 - Simple

My Mazes 48 - Simple

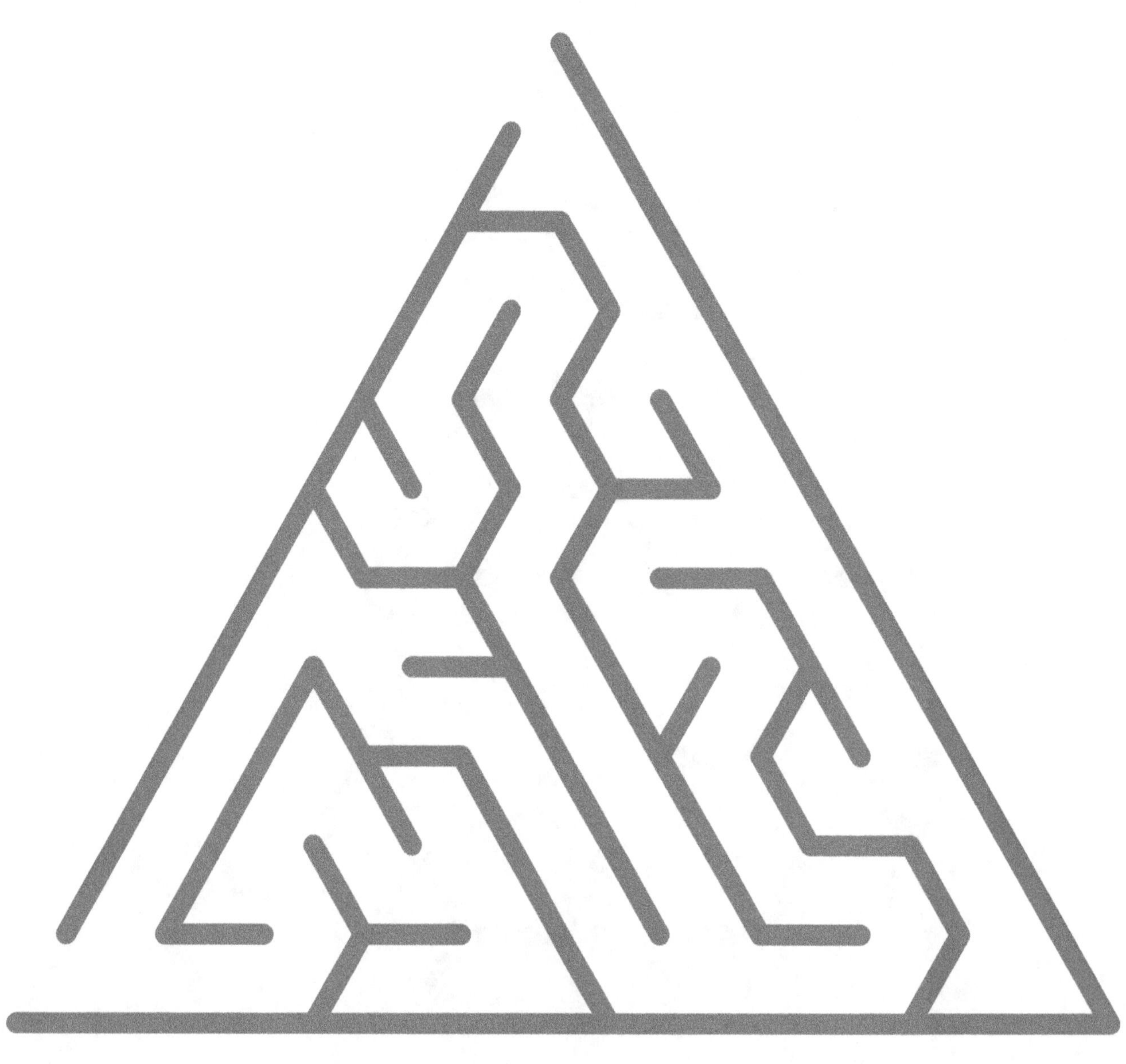

My Mazes 49 - Simple

My Mazes 50 - Simple

My Mazes 51 - Medium

My Mazes 52 - Simple

My Mazes 53 - Medium

My Mazes 54 - Medium

My Mazes 55 - Medium

My Mazes 56 - Medium

My Mazes 57 - Medium

My Mazes 58 - Simple

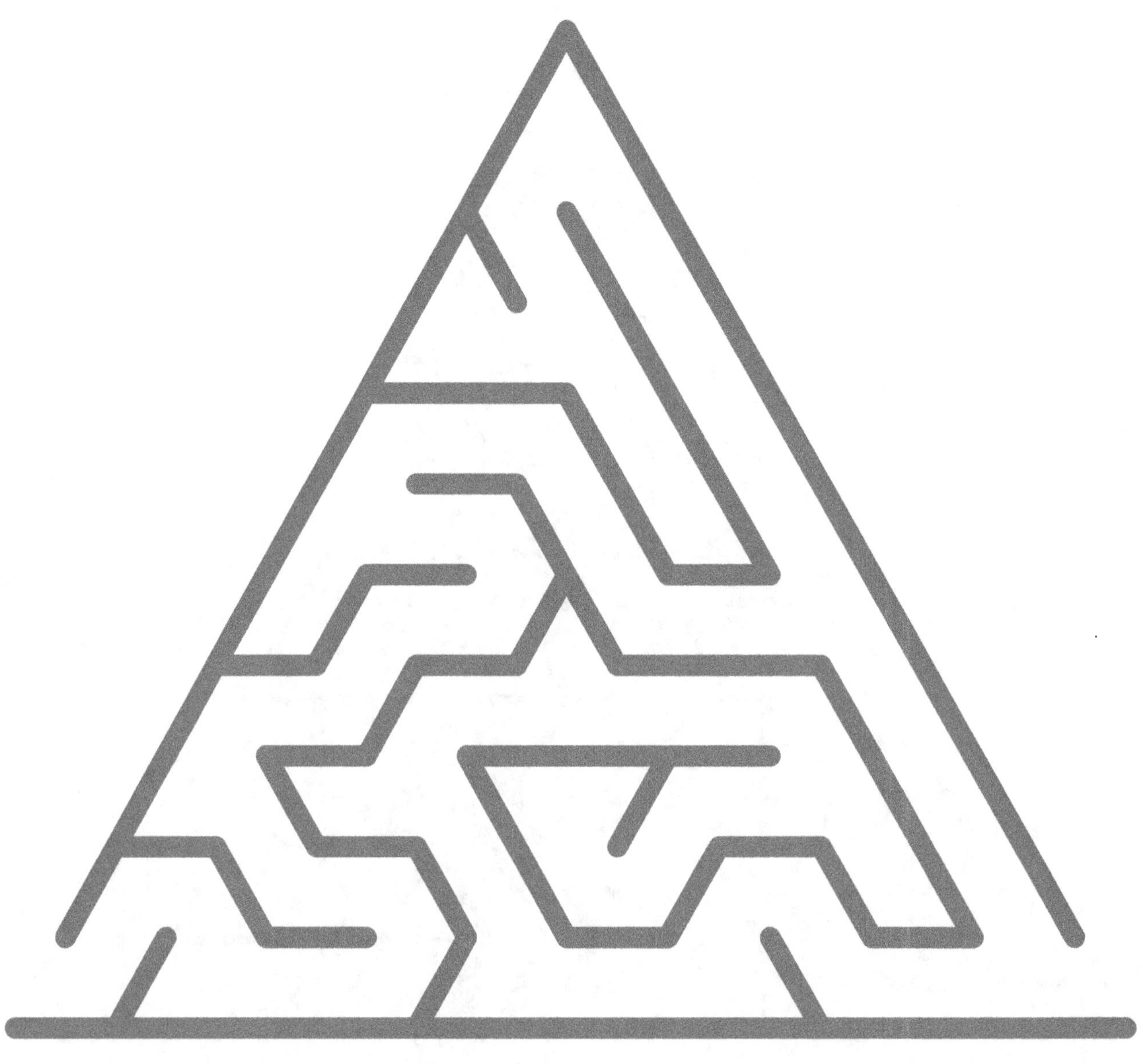

My Mazes 59 - Medium

My Mazes 60 - Medium

My Mazes 61 - Simple

My Mazes 62 - Simple

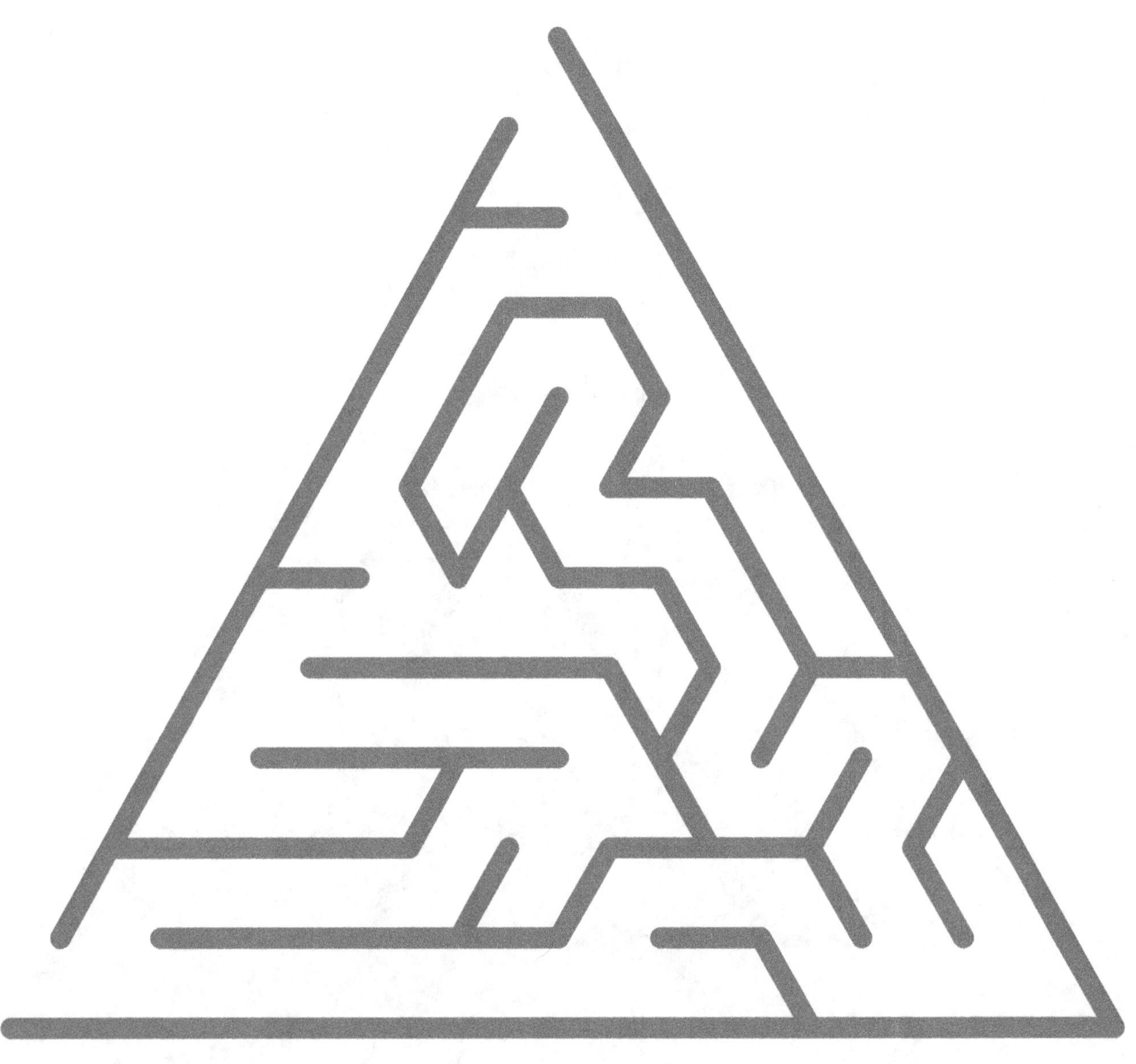

My Mazes 63 - Simple

My Mazes 64 - Simple

My Mazes 65 - Simple

My Mazes 66 - Simple

My Mazes 67 - Simple

My Mazes 68 - Medium

My Mazes 69 - Medium

My Mazes 70 - Simple

My Mazes 71 - Medium

My Mazes 72 - Medium

My Mazes 73 - Simple

My Mazes 74 - Medium

My Mazes 75 - Medium

My Mazes 76 - Medium

My Mazes 77 - Simple

My Mazes 78 - Simple

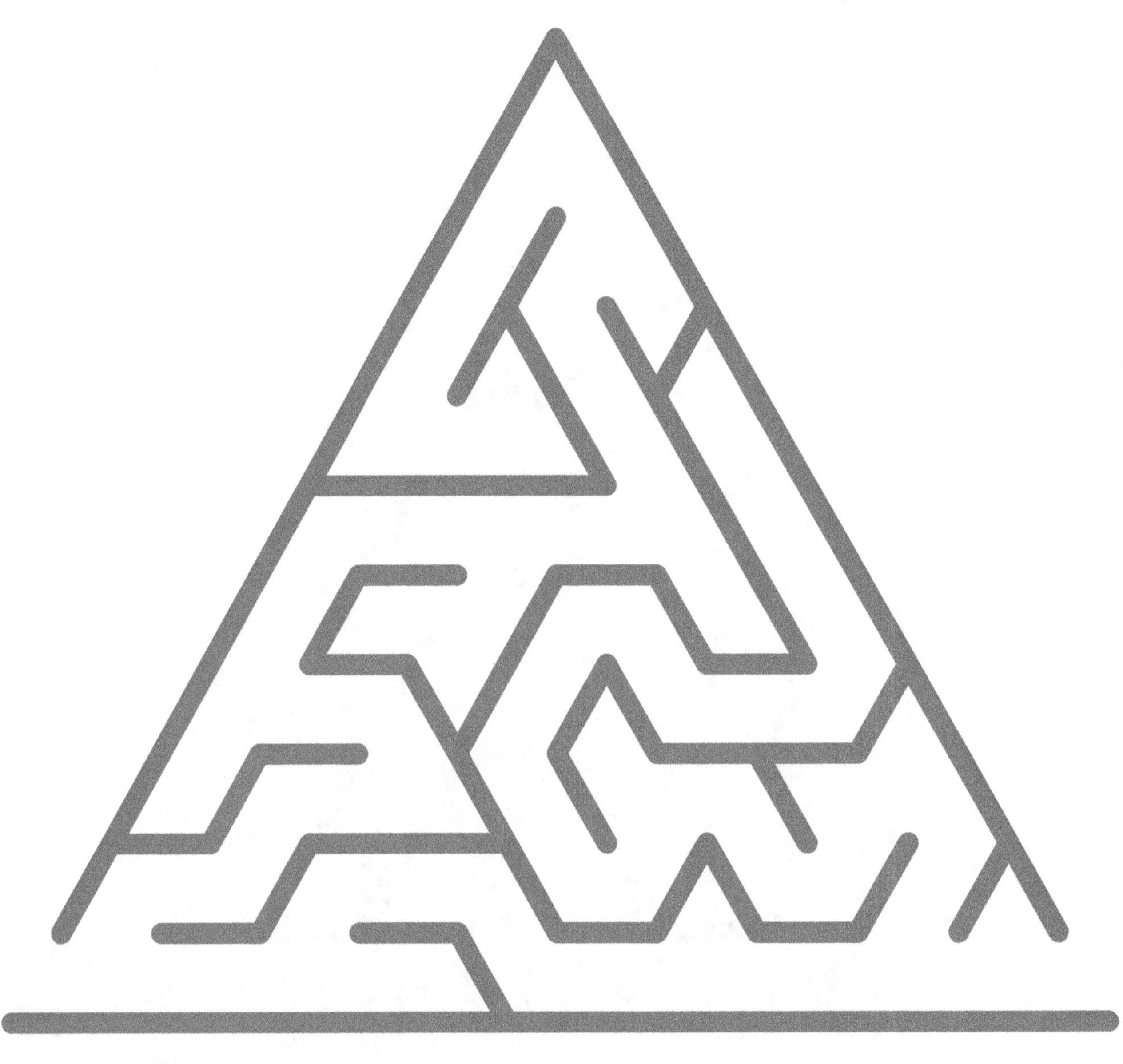

My Mazes 79 - Medium

My Mazes 80 - Medium

My Mazes 81 - Medium

My Mazes 82 - Simple

My Mazes 83 - Medium

My Mazes 84 - Medium

My Mazes 85 - Medium

My Mazes 86 - Medium

My Mazes 87 - Simple

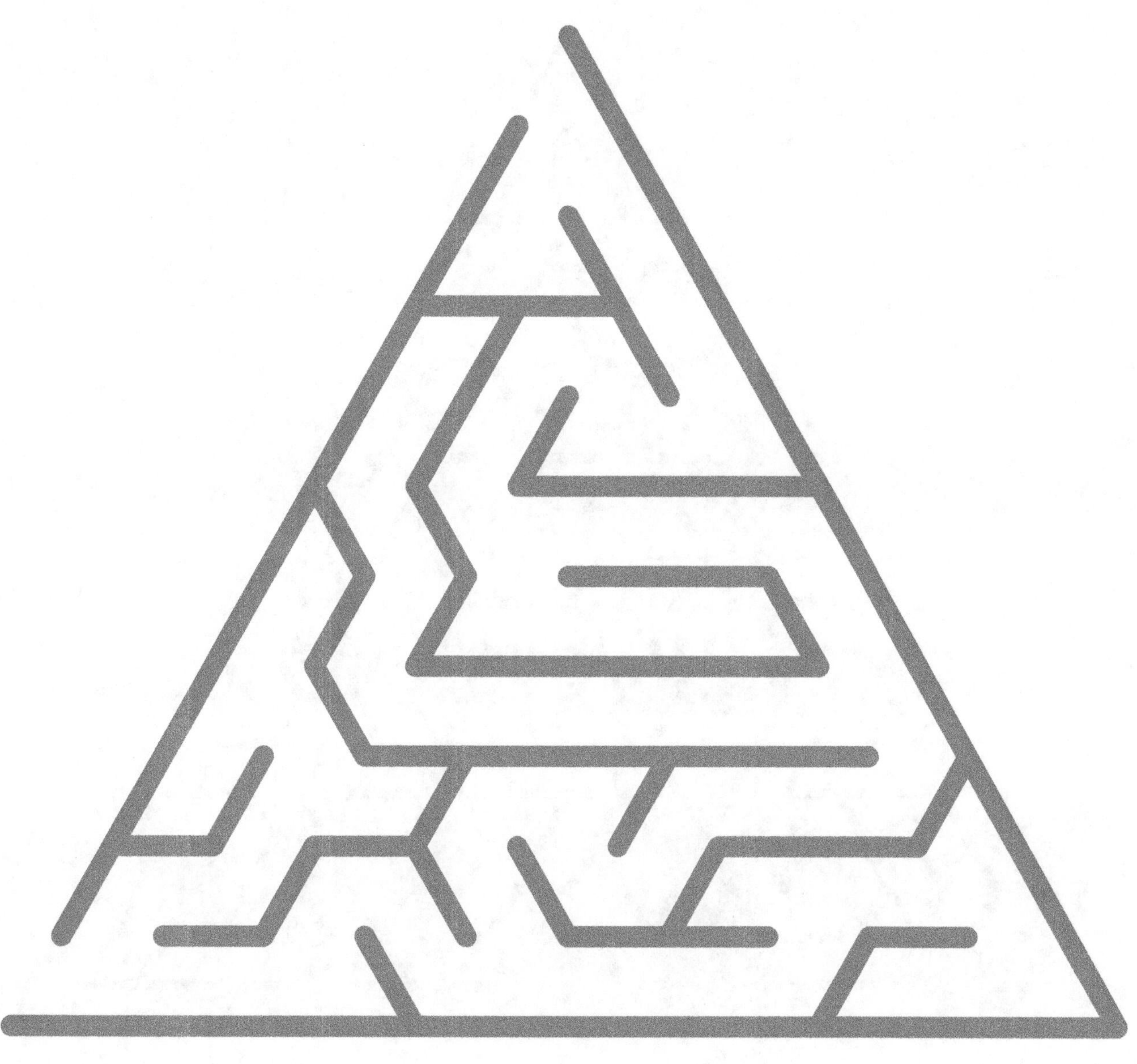

My Mazes 88 - Medium

My Mazes 89 - Simple

My Mazes 90 - Simple

My Mazes 91 - Simple

My Mazes 92 - Medium

My Mazes 93 - Medium

My Mazes 94 - Medium

My Mazes 95 - Medium

My Mazes 96 - Medium

My Mazes 97 - Simple

My Mazes 98 - Simple

My Mazes 99 - Medium

My Mazes 100 - Simple

My Mazes 101 - Medium

My Mazes 102 - Simple

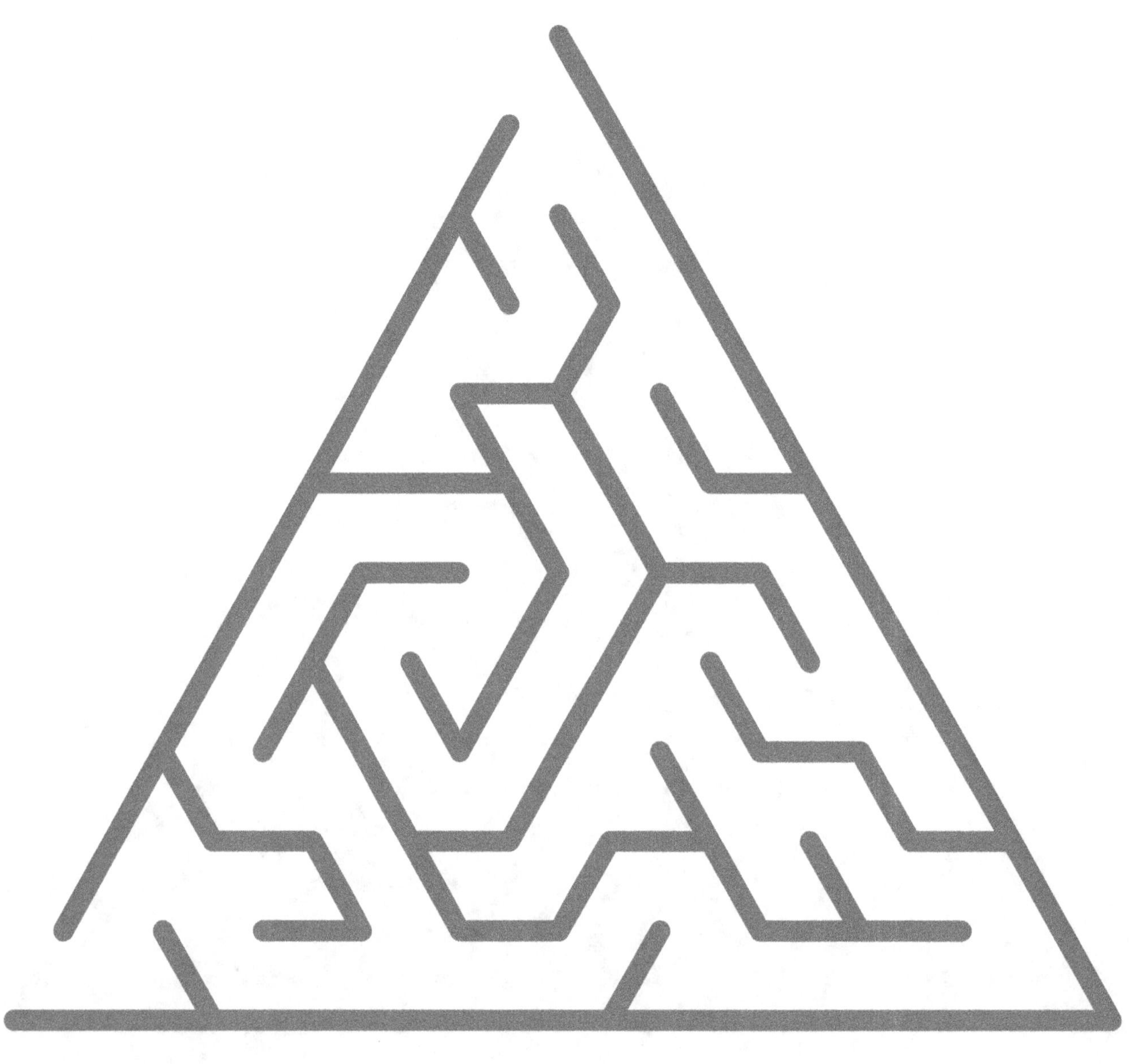

My Mazes 103 - Medium

My Mazes 104 - Medium

My Mazes 105 - Simple

My Mazes 106 - Medium

My Mazes 107 - Simple

My Mazes 108 - Medium

My Mazes 109 - Simple

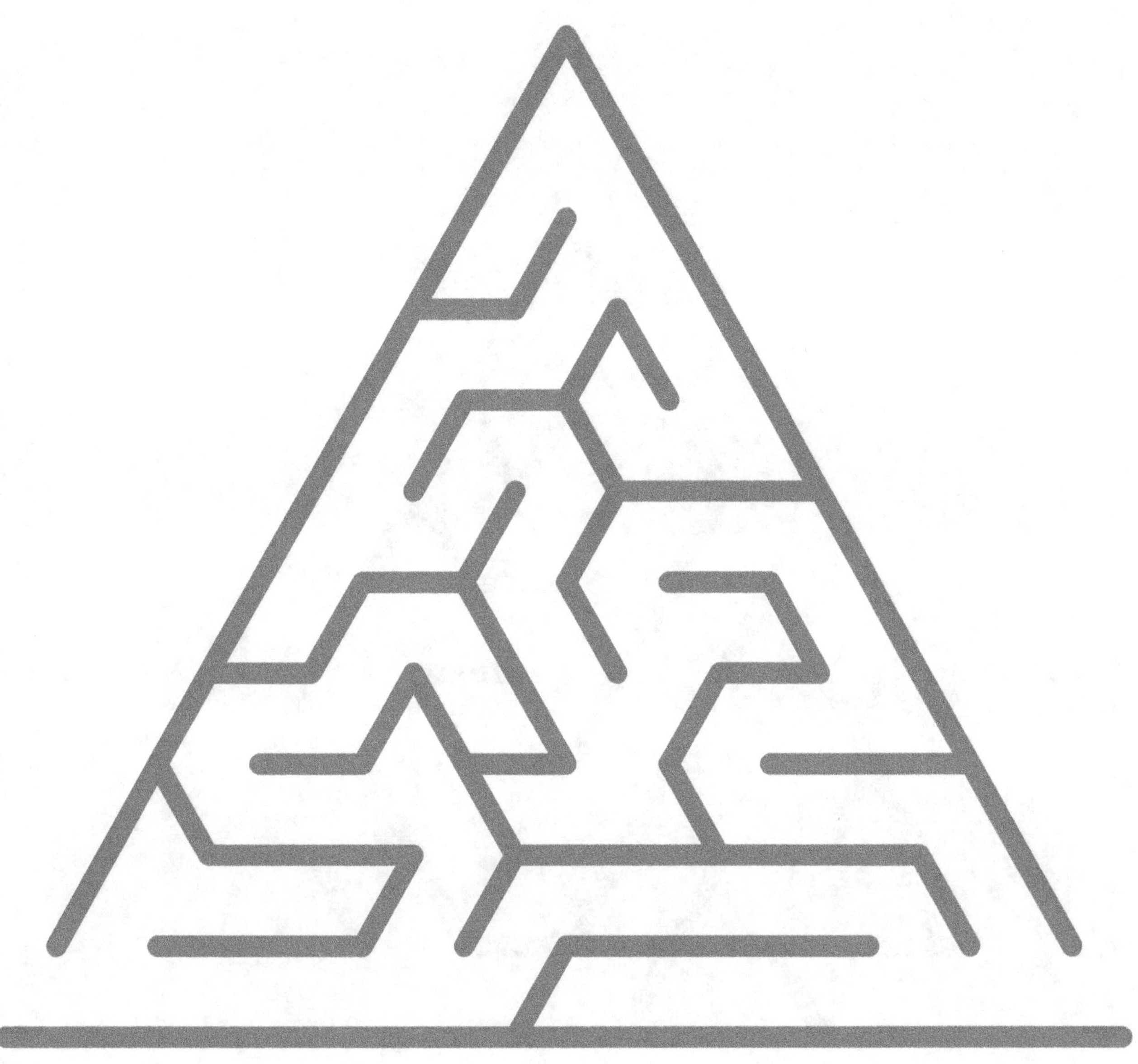

My Mazes 110 - Simple

My Mazes 111 - Simple

My Mazes 112 - Medium

My Mazes 113 - Medium

My Mazes 114 - Medium

My Mazes 115 - Simple

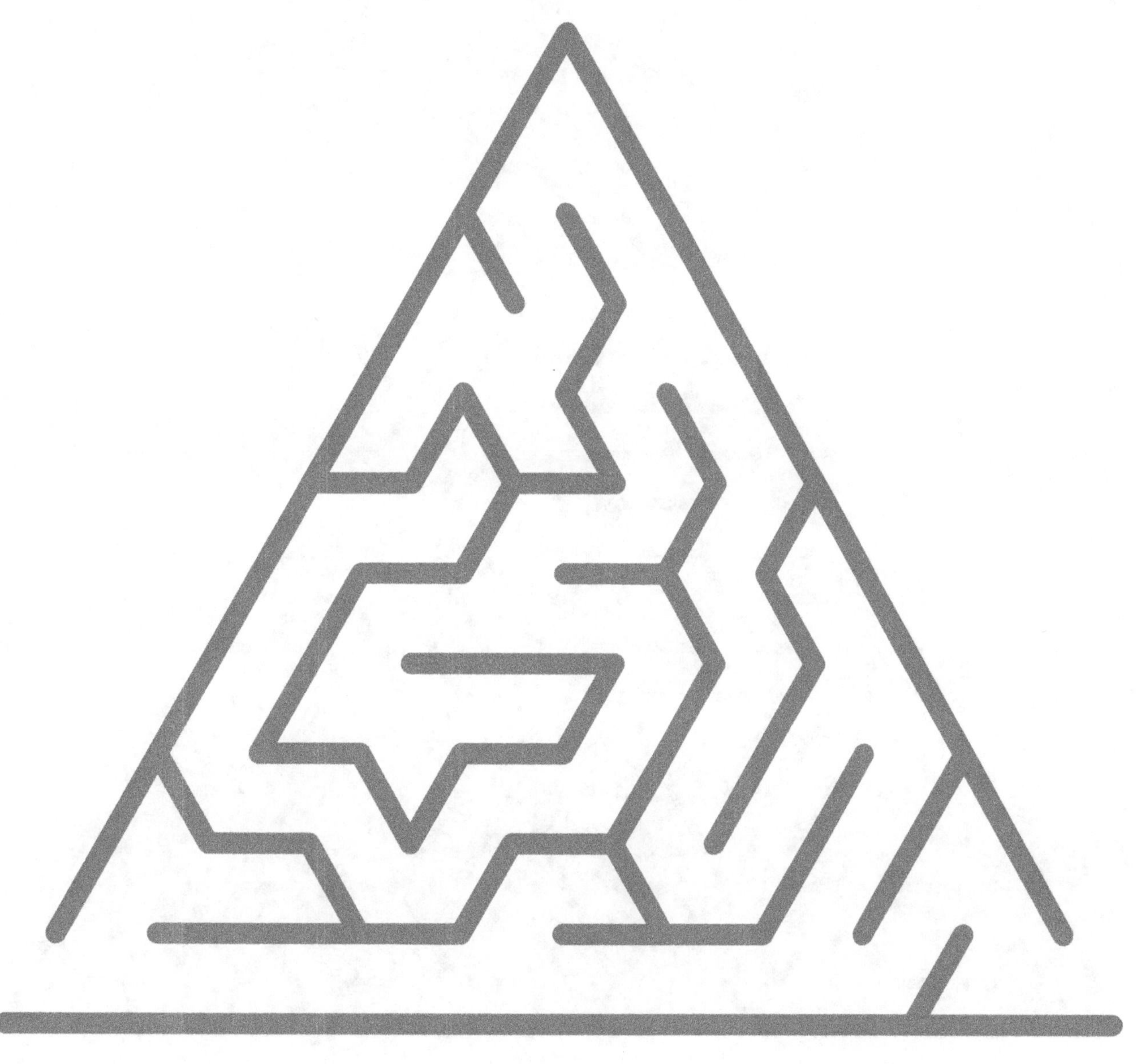

My Mazes 116 - Medium

My Mazes 117 - Simple

My Mazes 118 - Medium

My Mazes 119 - Medium

My Mazes 120 - Medium

My Mazes 121 - Medium

My Mazes 122 - Medium

My Mazes 123 - Medium

My Mazes 124 - Simple

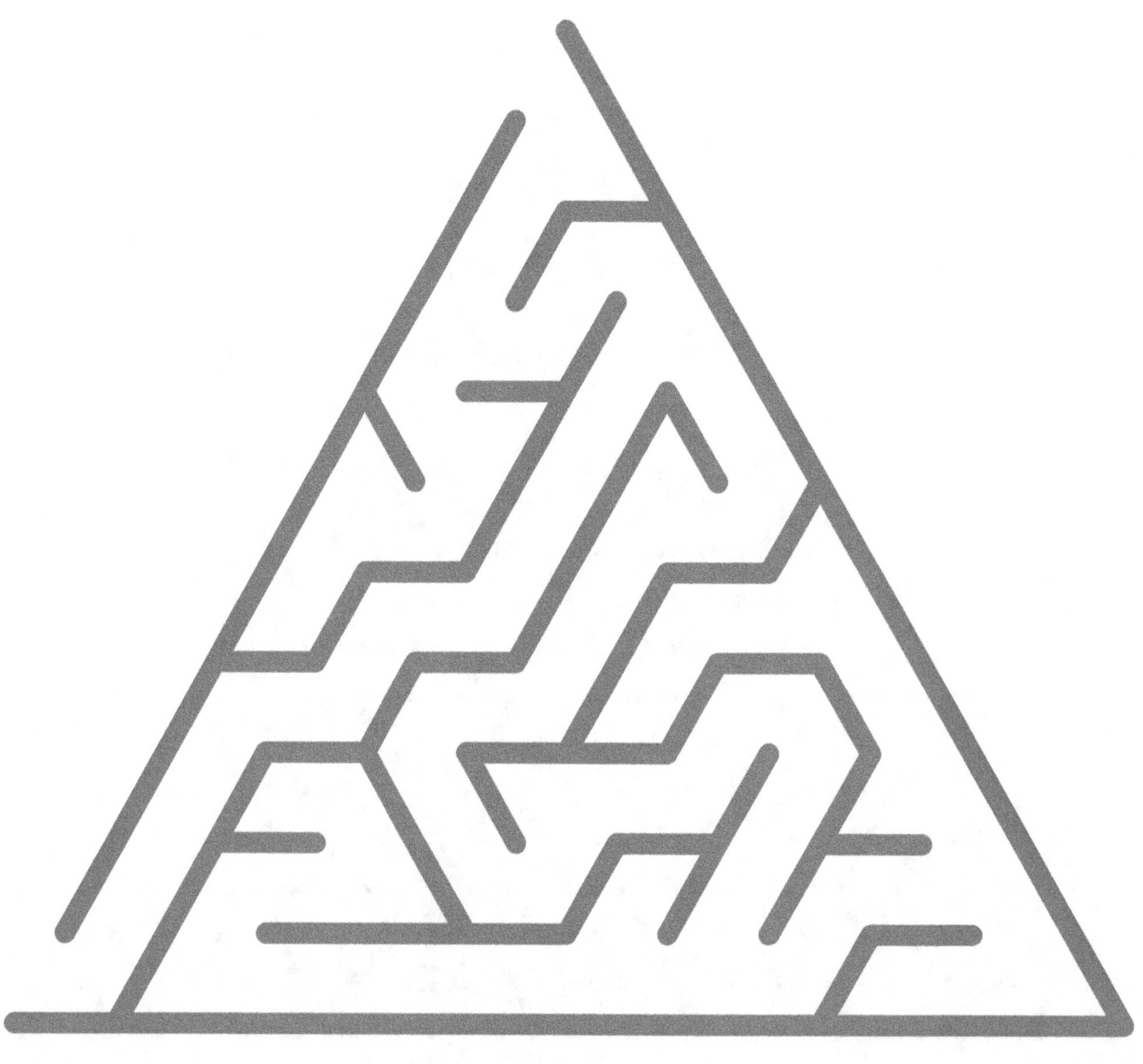

My Mazes 125 - Simple

My Mazes 126 - Medium

My Mazes 127 - Medium

My Mazes 128 - Simple

My Mazes 129 - Simple

My Mazes 130 - Medium

My Mazes 131 - Simple

My Mazes 132 - Simple

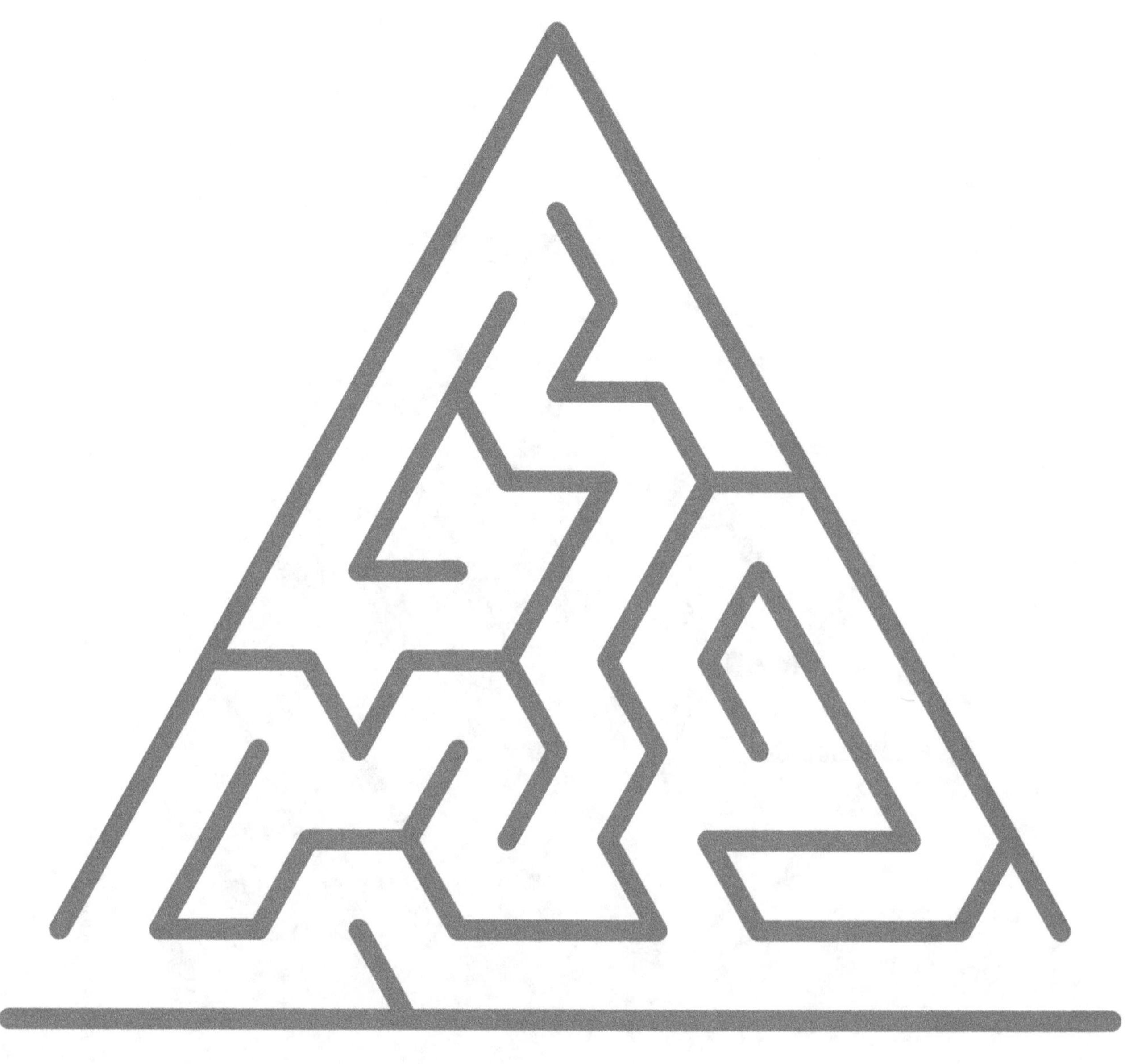

My Mazes 133 - Simple

My Mazes 134 - Medium

My Mazes 135 - Simple

My Mazes 136 - Medium

My Mazes 137 - Medium

My Mazes 138 - Medium

My Mazes 139 - Simple

My Mazes 140 - Medium

My Mazes 141 - Simple

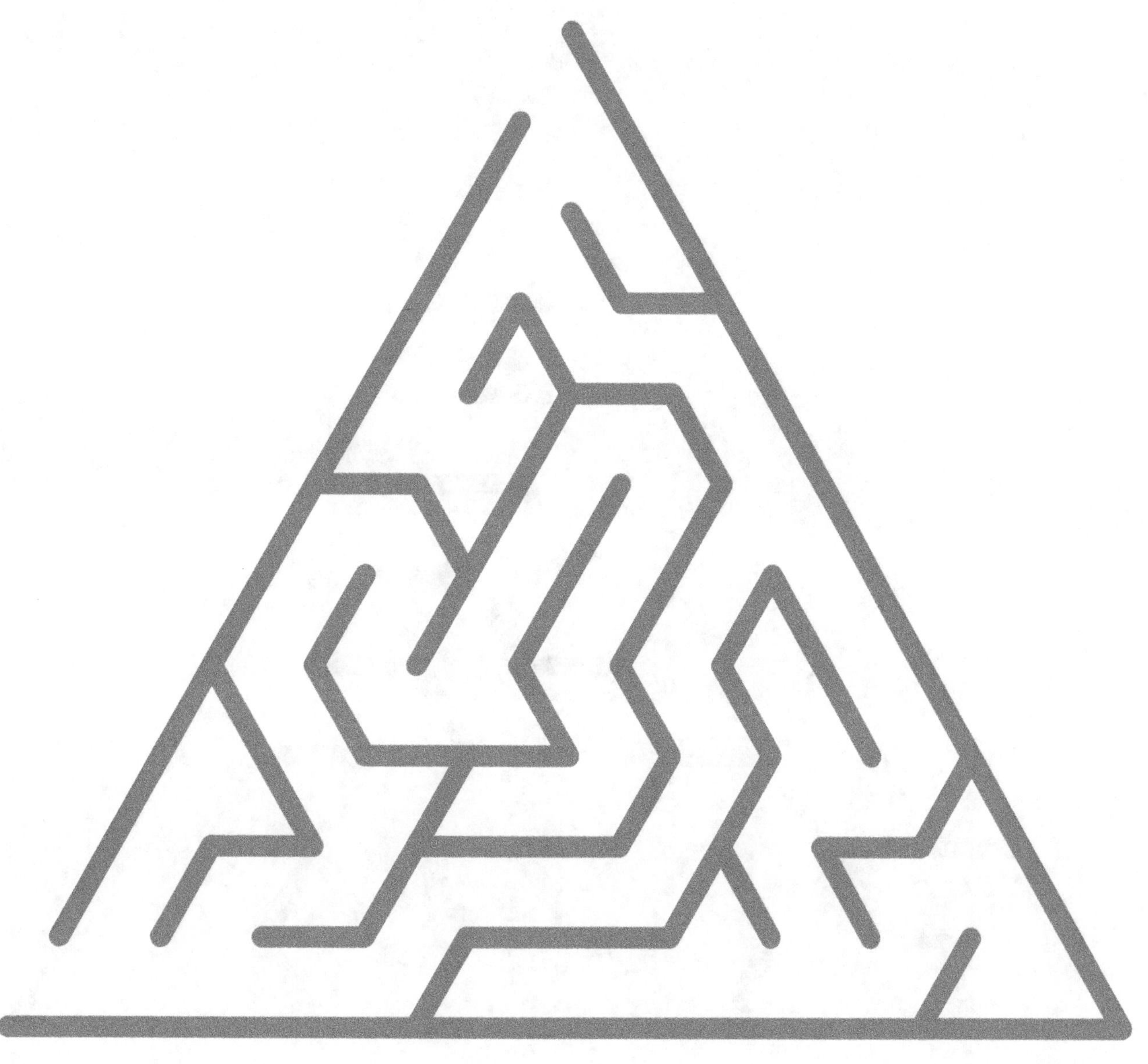

My Mazes 142 - Simple

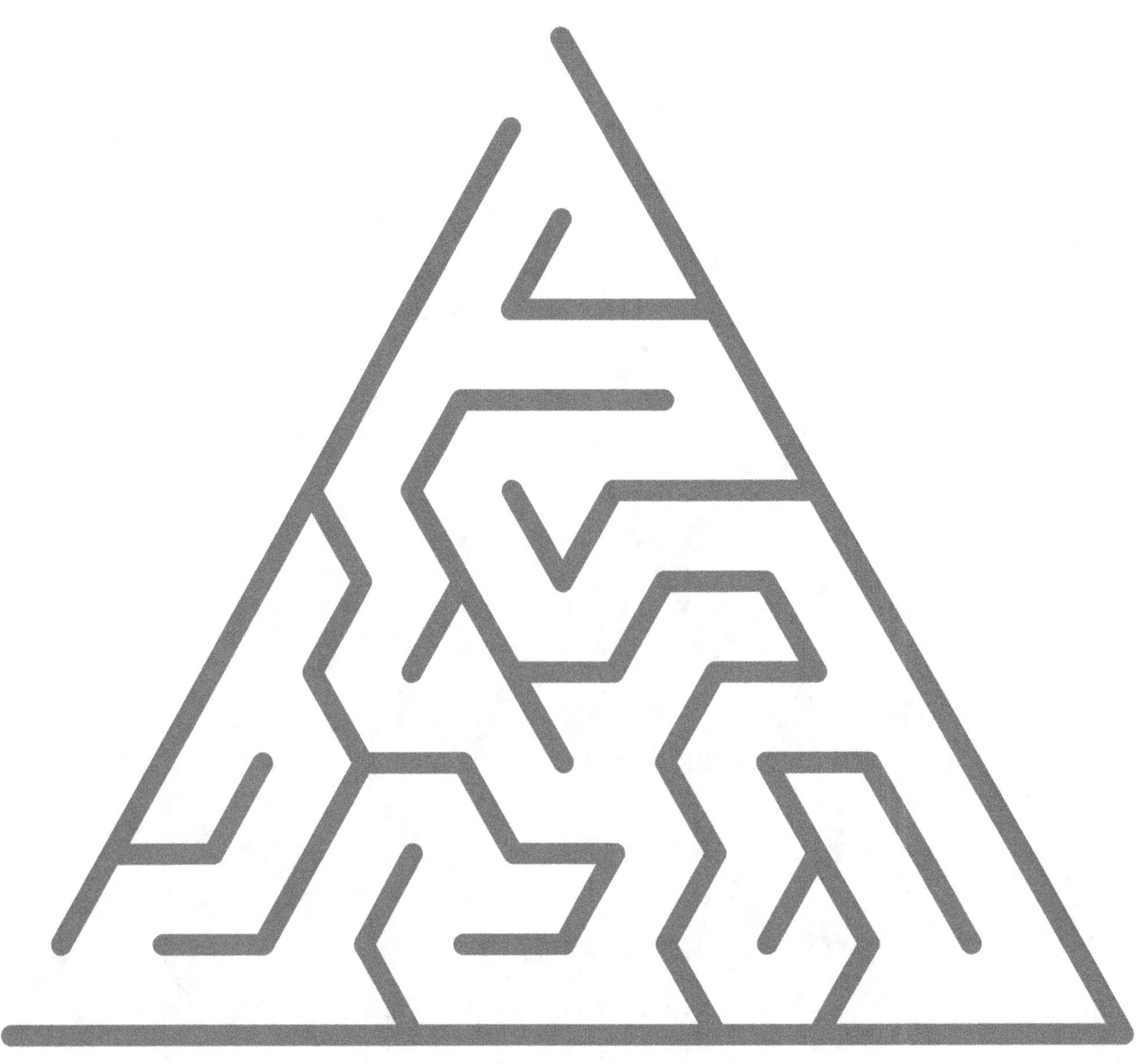

My Mazes 143 - Simple

My Mazes 144 - Simple

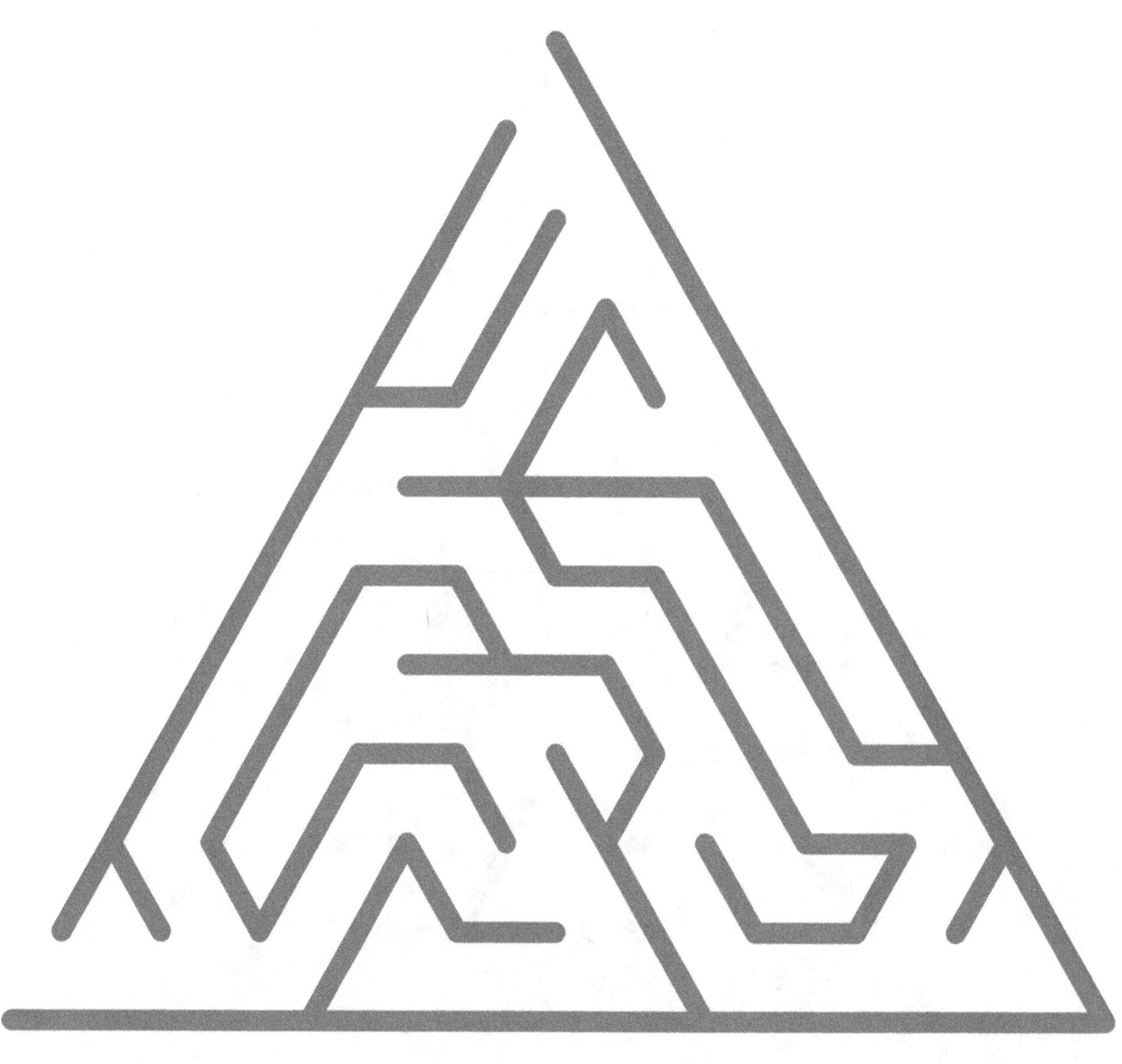

My Mazes 145 - Simple

My Mazes 146 - Simple

My Mazes 147 - Medium

My Mazes 148 - Simple

My Mazes 149 - Simple

My Mazes 150 - Simple

My Mazes 151 - Simple

My Mazes 152 - Simple

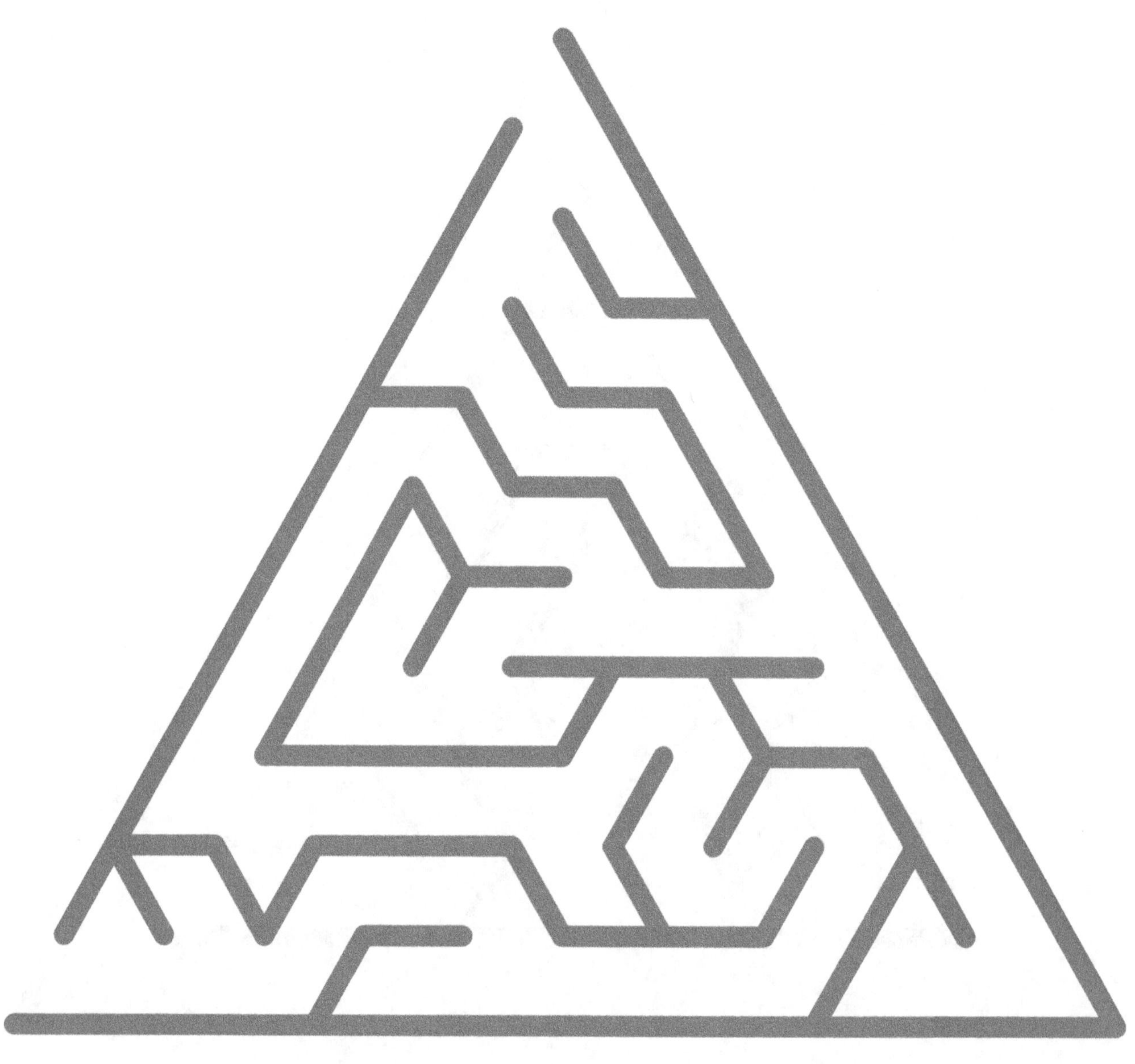

My Mazes 153 - Simple

My Mazes 154 - Simple

My Mazes 155 - Medium

My Mazes 156 - Medium

My Mazes 157 - Medium

My Mazes 158 - Simple

My Mazes 159 - Medium

My Mazes 160 - Medium

My Mazes 161 - Simple

My Mazes 162 - Simple

My Mazes 163 - Medium

My Mazes 164 - Medium

My Mazes 165 - Medium

My Mazes 166 - Simple

My Mazes 167 - Simple

My Mazes 168 - Medium

My Mazes 169 - Medium

My Mazes 170 - Medium

My Mazes 171 - Medium

My Mazes 172 - Medium

My Mazes 173 - Medium

My Mazes 174 - Simple

My Mazes 175 - Medium

My Mazes 176 - Simple

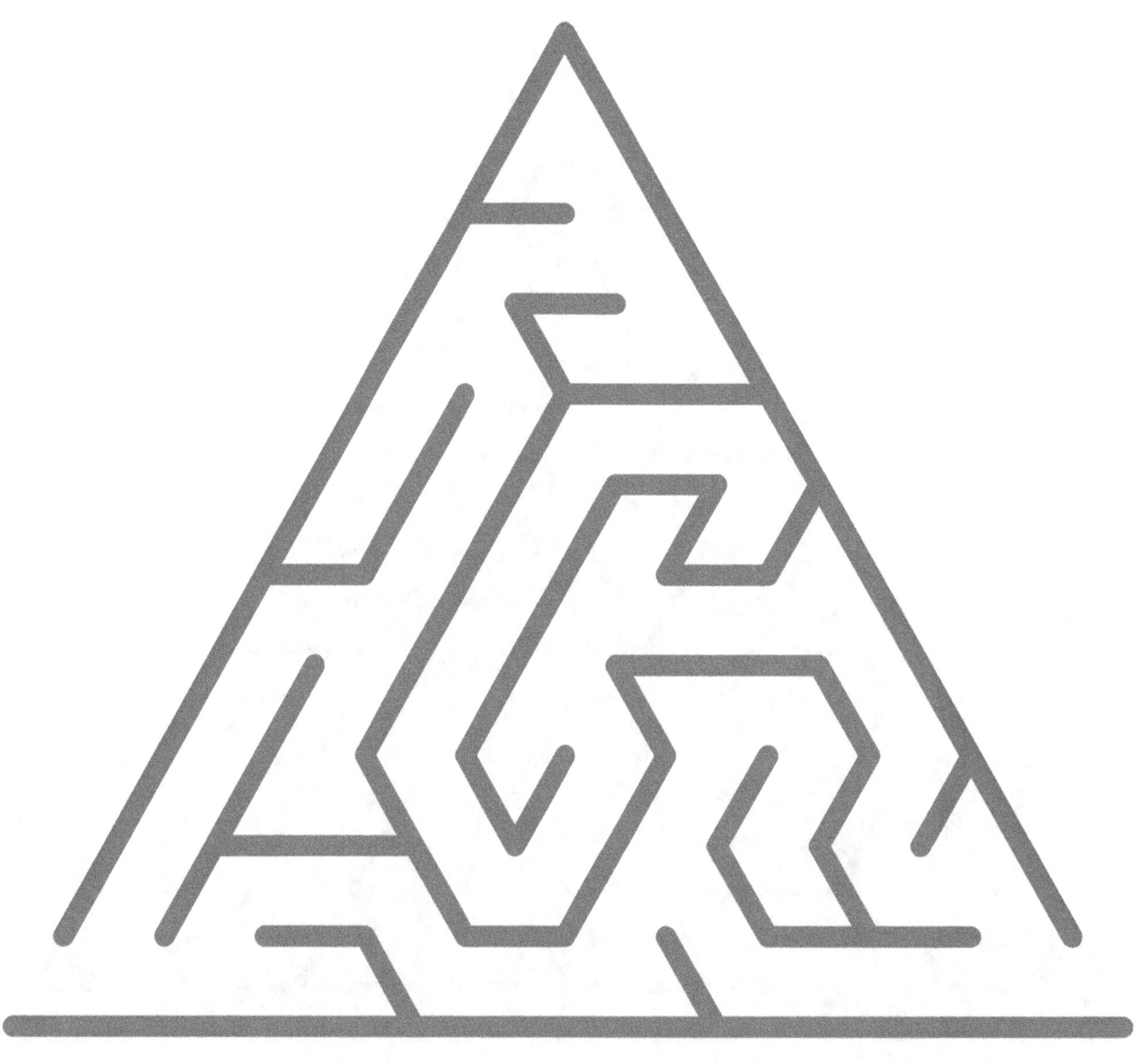

My Mazes 177 - Simple

My Mazes 178 - Simple

My Mazes 179 - Simple

My Mazes 180 - Medium

My Mazes 181 - Medium

My Mazes 182 - Medium

My Mazes 183 - Simple

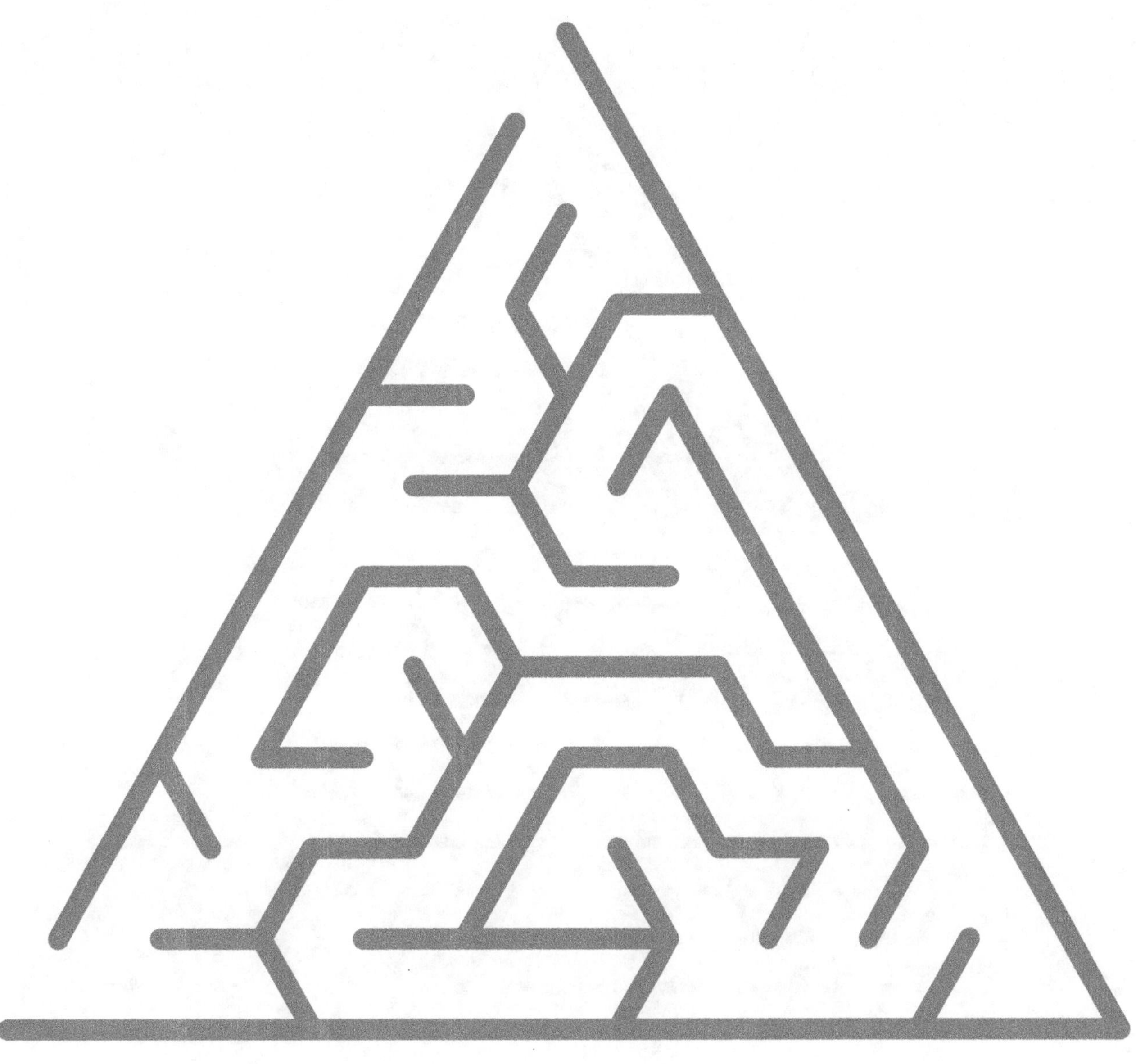

My Mazes 184 - Medium

My Mazes 185 - Simple

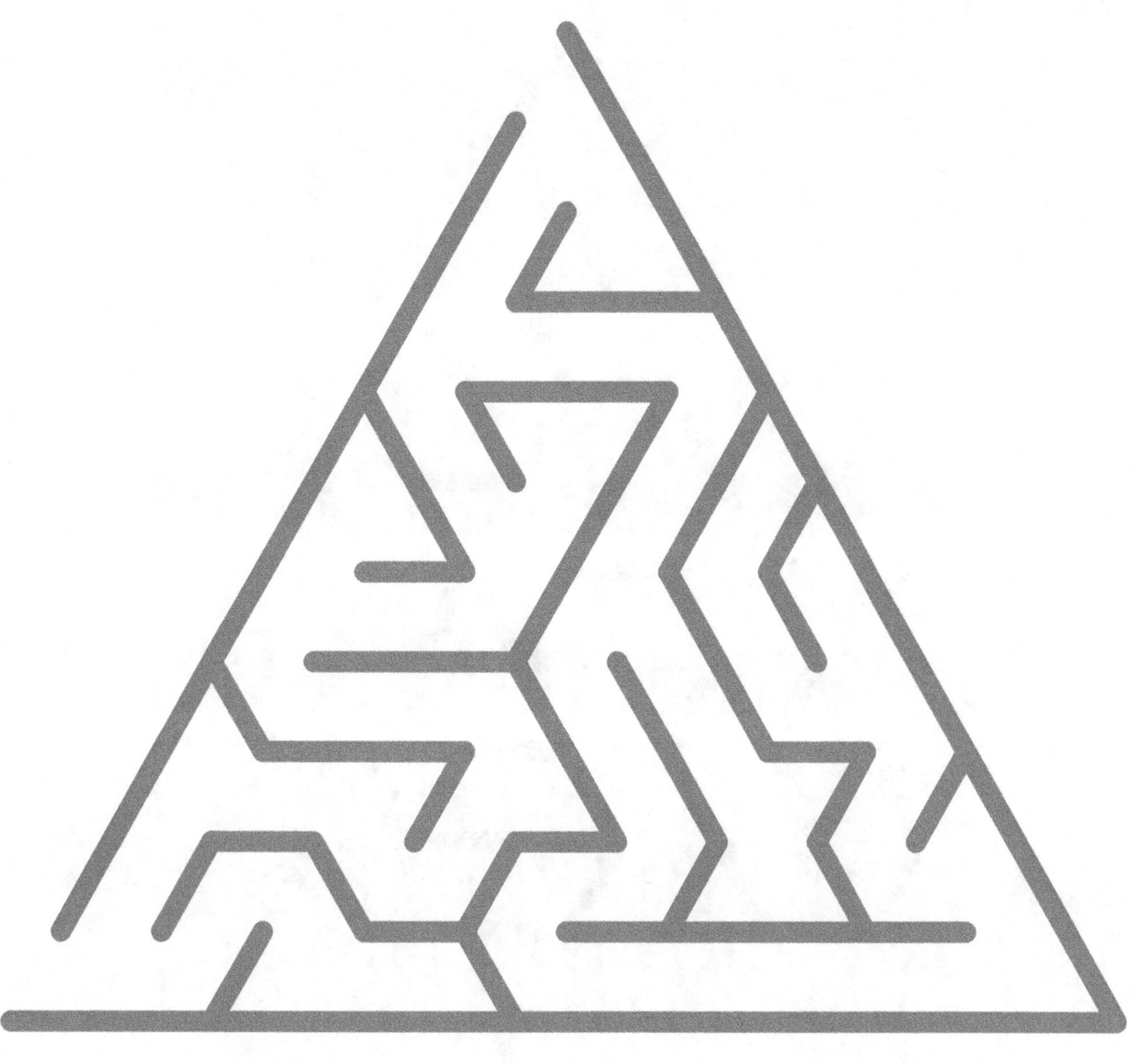

My Mazes 186 - Simple

My Mazes 187 - Simple

My Mazes 188 - Simple

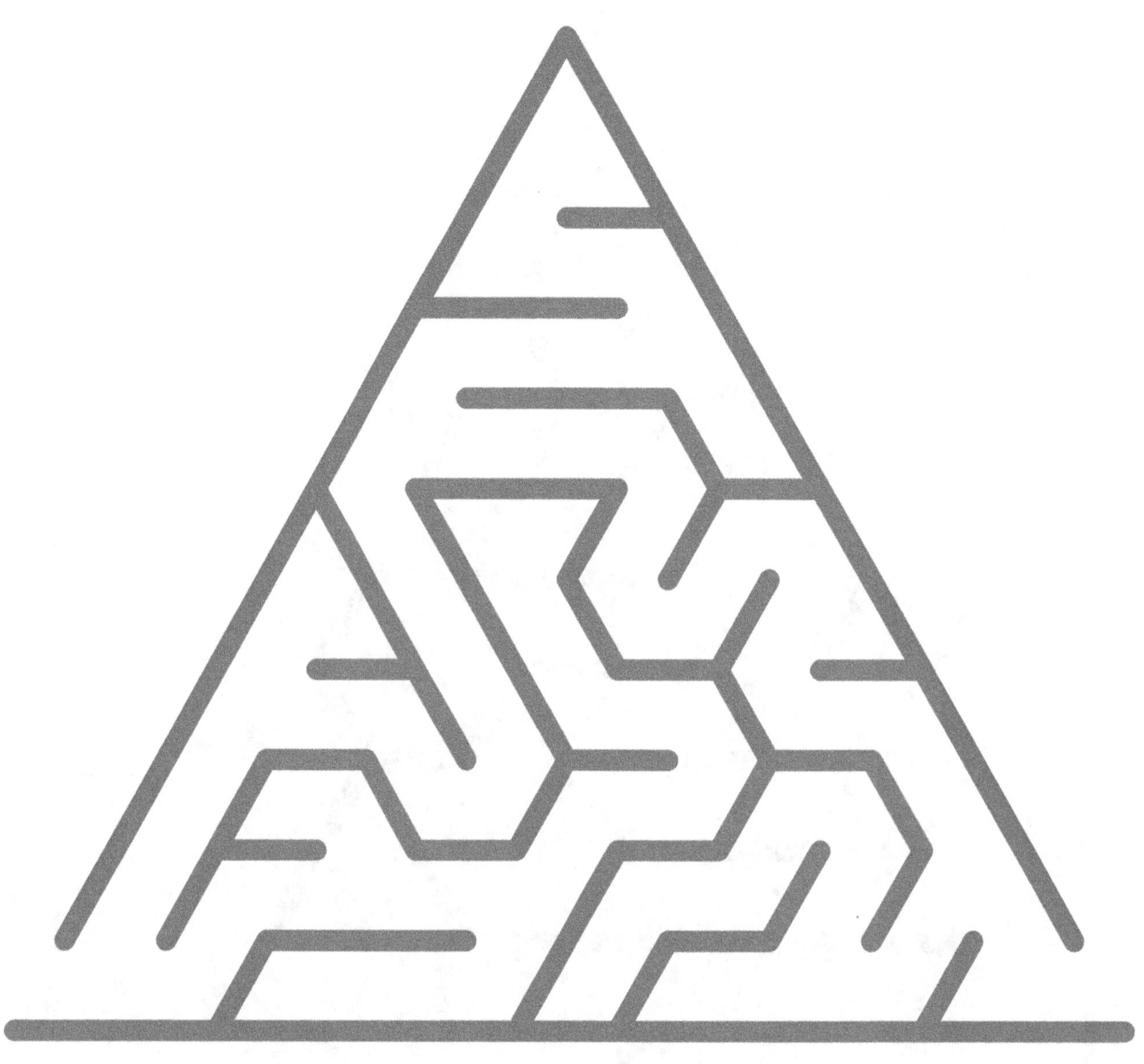

My Mazes 189 - Medium

My Mazes 190 - Medium

My Mazes 191 - Medium

My Mazes 192 - Medium

My Mazes 193 - Simple

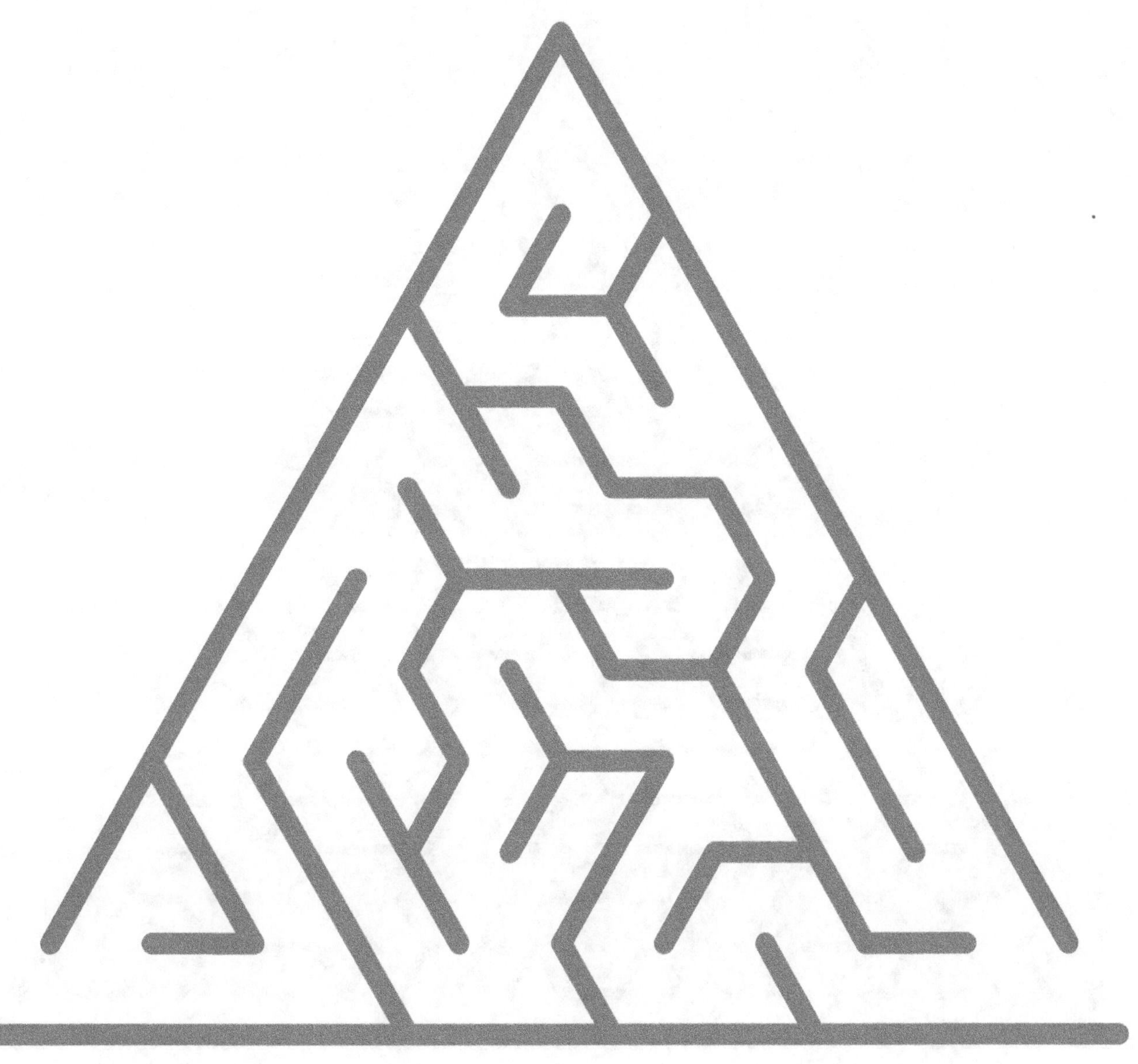

My Mazes 194 - Medium

My Mazes 195 - Simple

My Mazes 196 - Medium

My Mazes 197 - Simple

My Mazes 198 - Simple

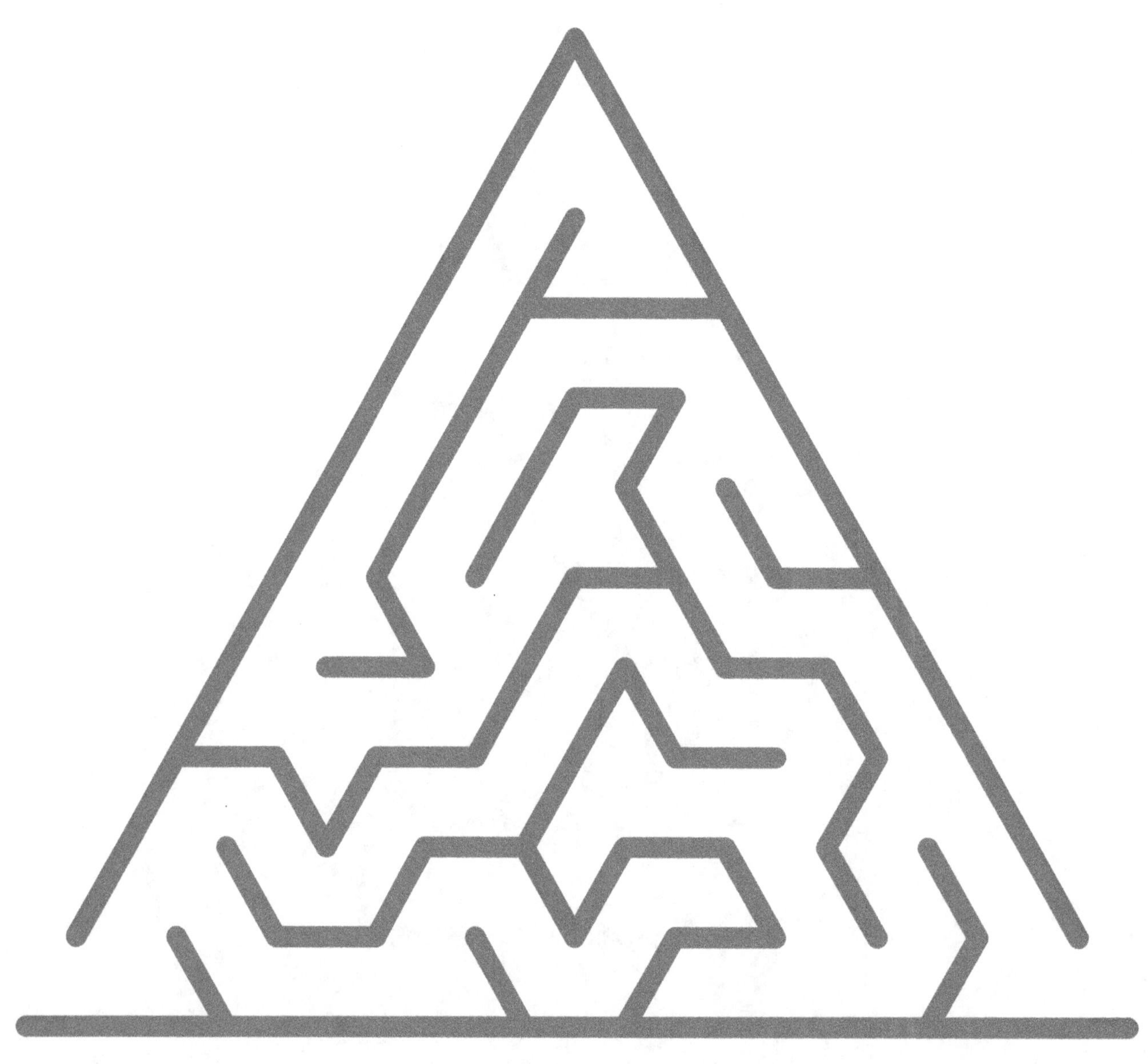

My Mazes 199 - Simple

My Mazes 200 - Medium

Page 1-1

Page 2-1

Page 3-1

Page 4-1

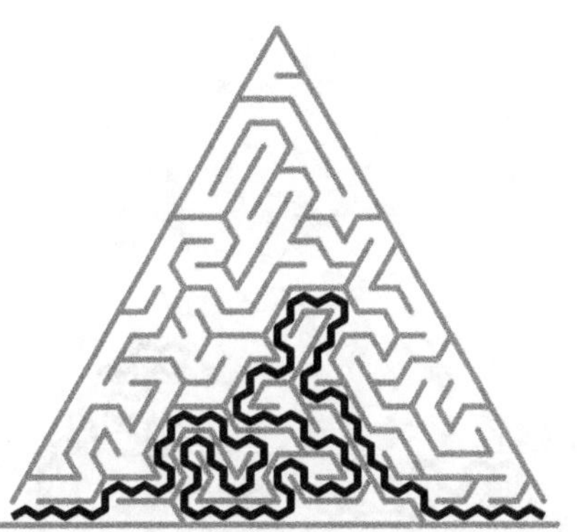

Page 5-1

Page 6-1

Page 7-1

Page 8-1

Page 9-1

Page 10-1

Page 11-1

Page 12-1

Page 13-1

Page 14-1

Page 15-1

Page 16-1

Page 17-1

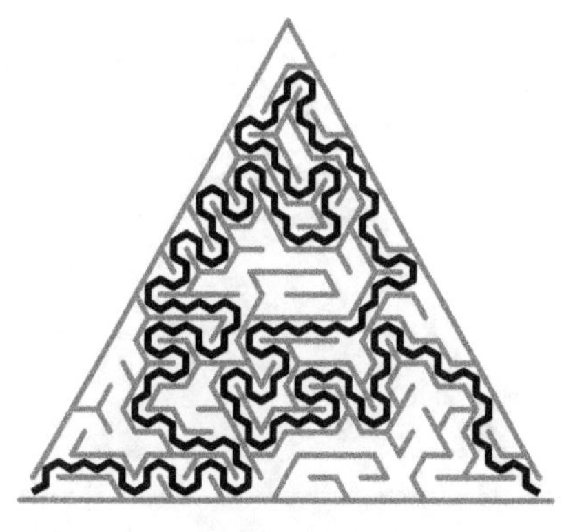

Page 18-1

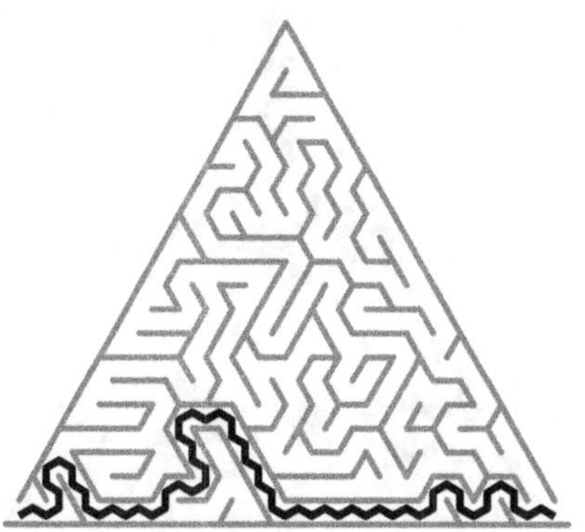

Page 19-1

Page 20-1

Page 21-1

Page 22-1

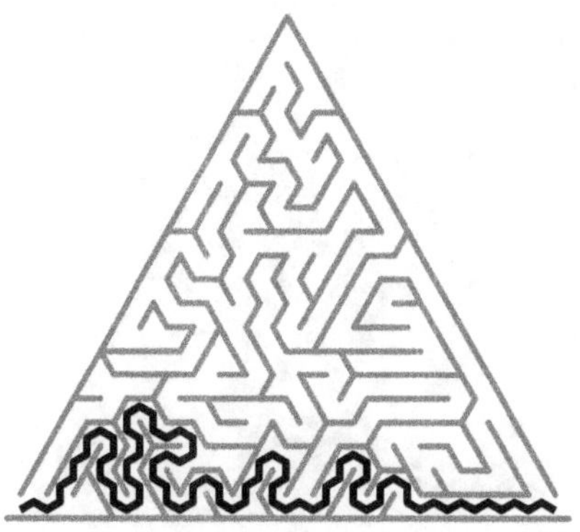

Page 23-1

Page 24-1

Page 25-1

Page 26-1

Page 27-1

Page 28-1

Page 29-1

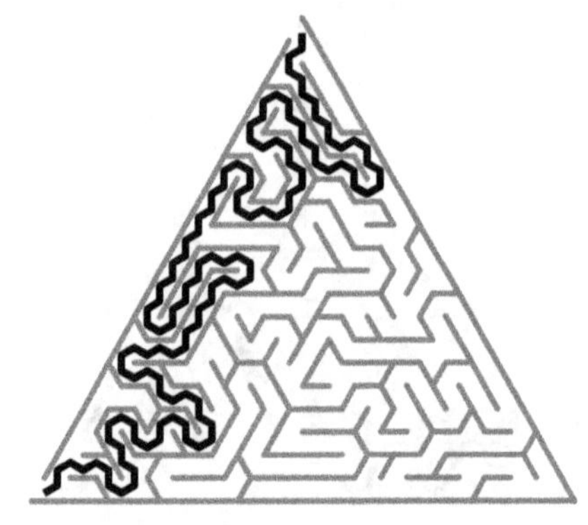

Page 30-1

Page 31-1

Page 32-1

Page 33-1

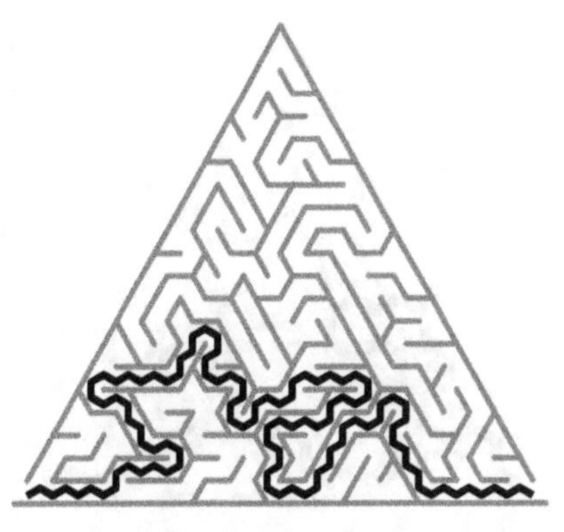

Page 34-1

Page 35-1

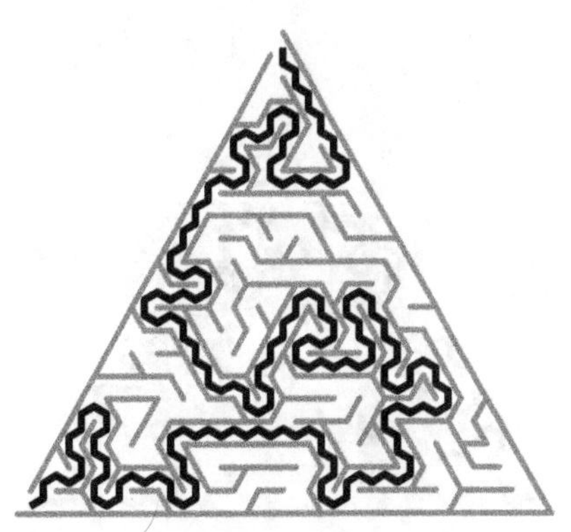

Page 36-1

Page 37-1

Page 38-1

Page 39-1

Page 40-1

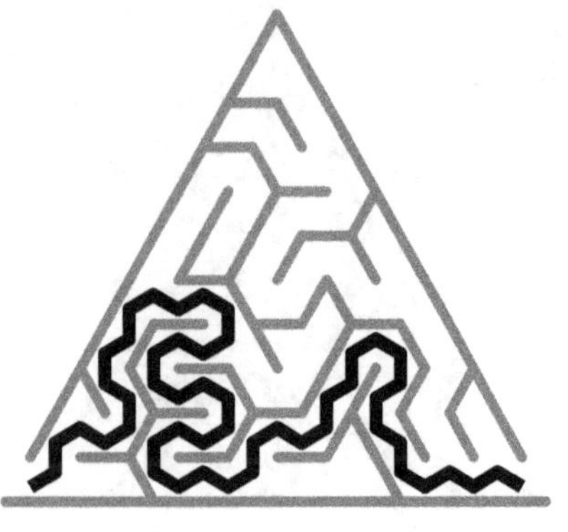

Page 41-1

Page 42-1

Page 43-1

Page 44-1

Page 45-1

Page 46-1

Page 47-1

Page 48-1

Page 49-1

Page 50-1

Page 51-1

Page 52-1

Page 53-1

Page 54-1

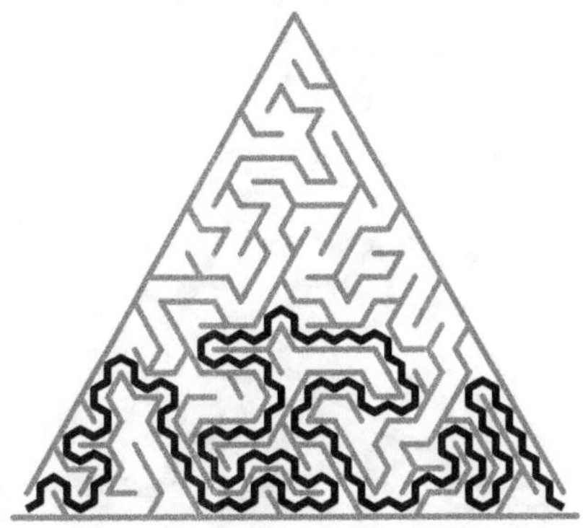

Page 55-1

Page 56-1

Page 57-1

Page 58-1

Page 59-1

Page 60-1

Page 61-1

Page 62-1

Page 63-1

Page 64-1

Page 65-1

Page 66-1

Page 67-1

Page 68-1

Page 69-1

Page 70-1

Page 71-1

Page 72-1

Page 73-1

Page 74-1

Page 75-1

Page 76-1

Page 77-1

Page 78-1

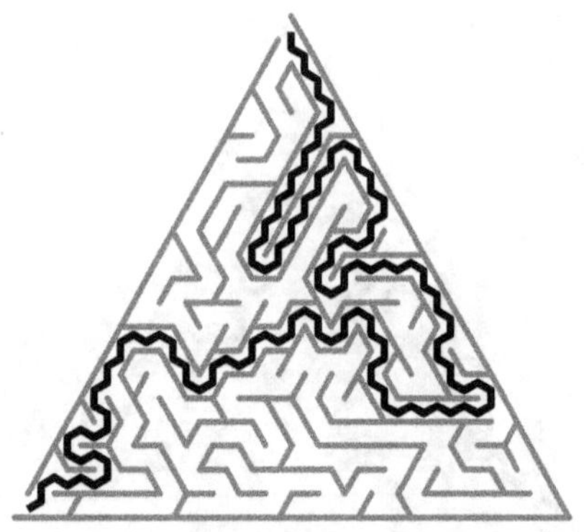

Page 79-1

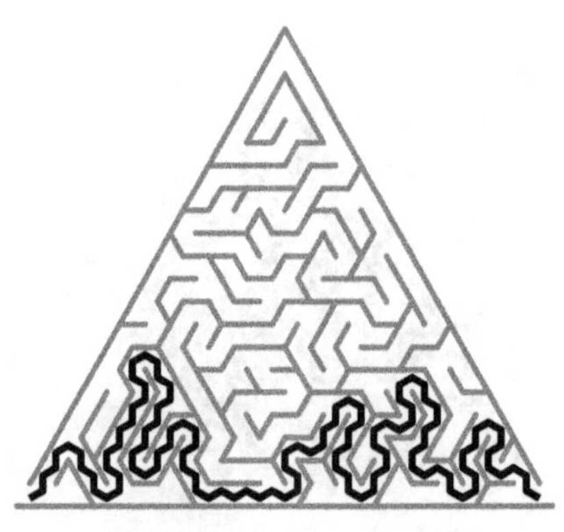

Page 80-1

Page 81-1

Page 82-1

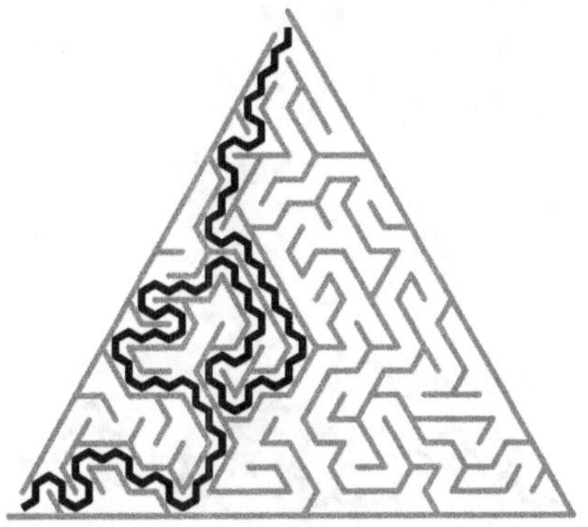

Page 83-1

Page 84-1

Page 85-1

Page 86-1

Page 87-1

Page 88-1

Page 89-1

Page 90-1

Page 91-1

Page 92-1

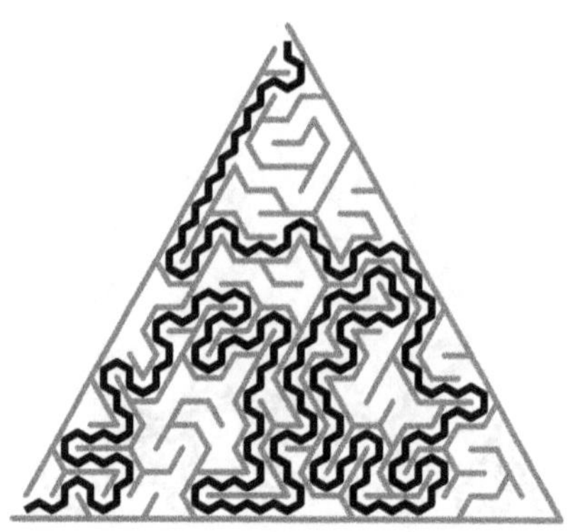

Page 93-1

Page 94-1

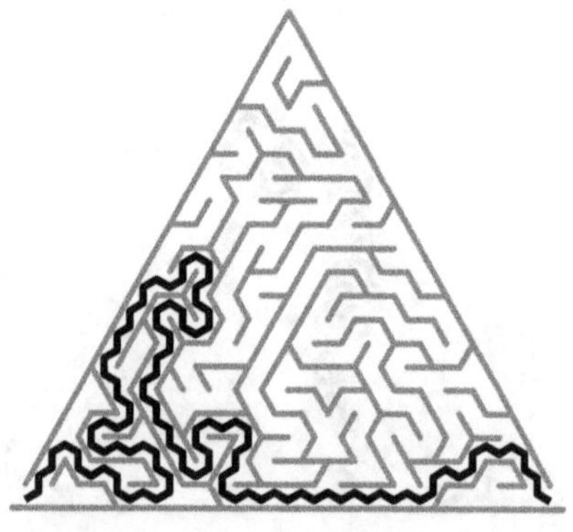

Page 95-1

Page 96-1

Page 97-1

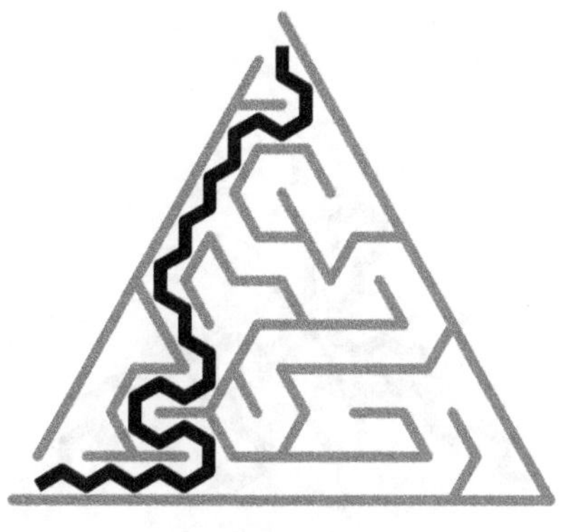

Page 98-1

Page 99-1

Page 100-1

Page 101-1

Page 102-1

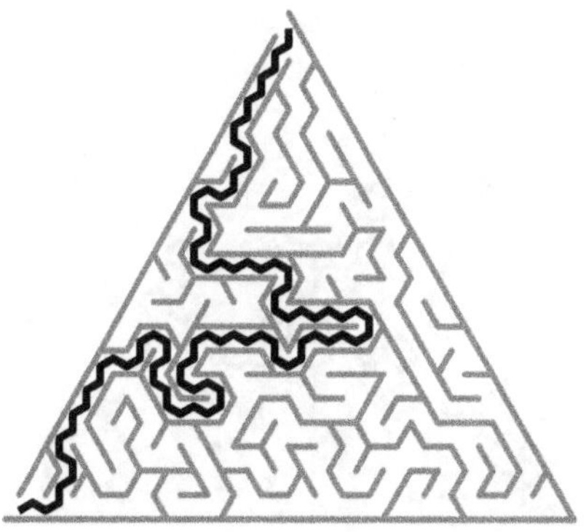

Page 103-1

Page 104-1

Page 105-1

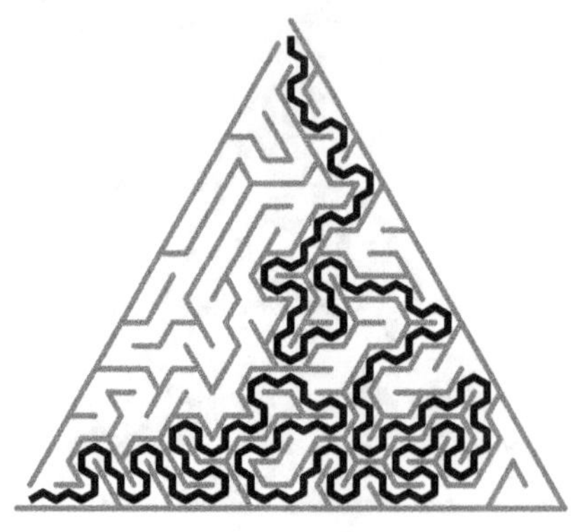

Page 106-1

Page 107-1

Page 108-1

Page 109-1

Page 110-1

Page 111-1

Page 112-1

Page 113-1

Page 114-1

Page 115-1

Page 116-1

Page 117-1

Page 118-1

Page 119-1

Page 120-1

Page 121-1

Page 122-1

Page 123-1

Page 124-1

Page 125-1

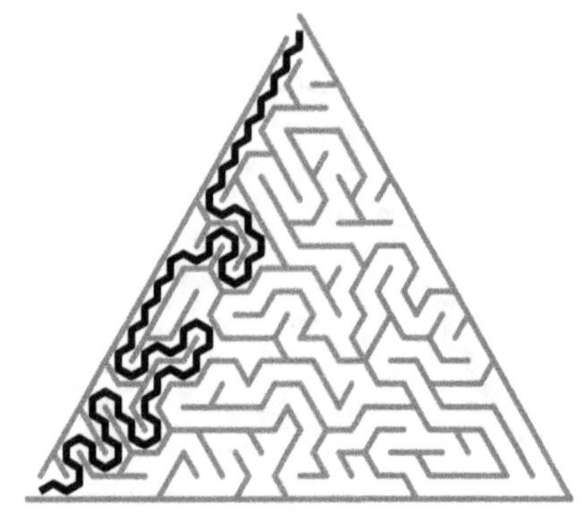

Page 126-1

Page 127-1

Page 128-1

Page 129-1

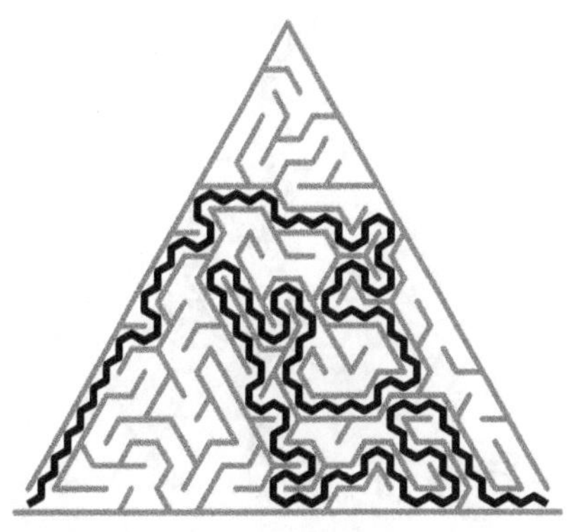

Page 130-1

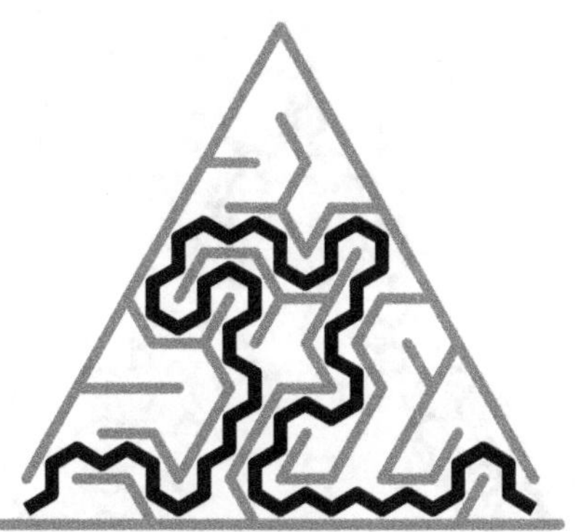

Page 131-1

Page 132-1

Page 133-1

Page 134-1

Page 135-1

Page 136-1

Page 137-1

Page 138-1

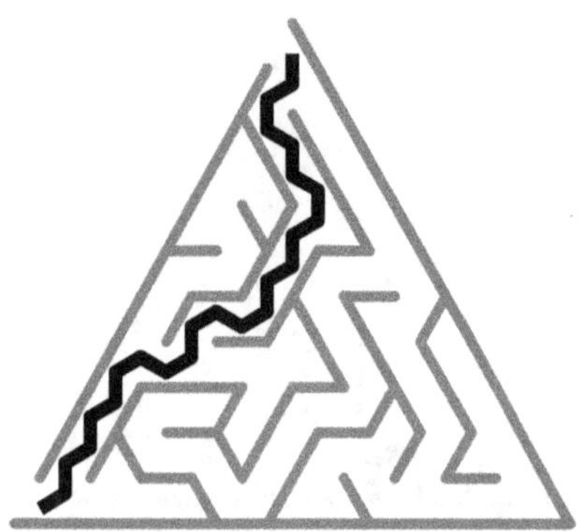

Page 139-1

Page 140-1

Page 141-1

Page 142-1

Page 143-1

Page 144-1

Page 145-1

Page 146-1

Page 147-1

Page 148-1

Page 149-1

Page 150-1

Page 151-1

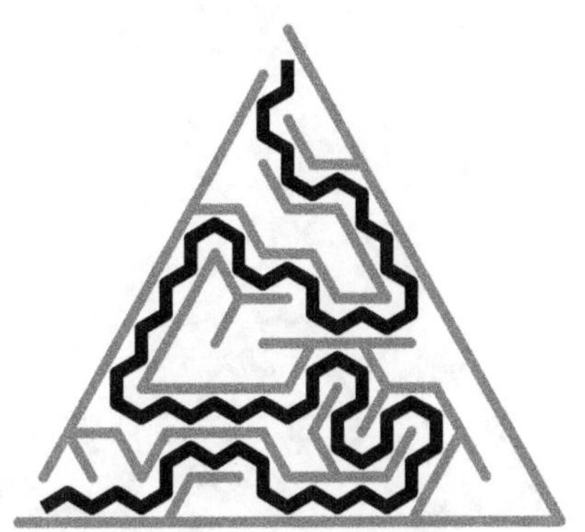

Page 152-1

Page 153-1

Page 154-1

Page 155-1

Page 156-1

Page 157-1

Page 158-1

Page 159-1

Page 160-1

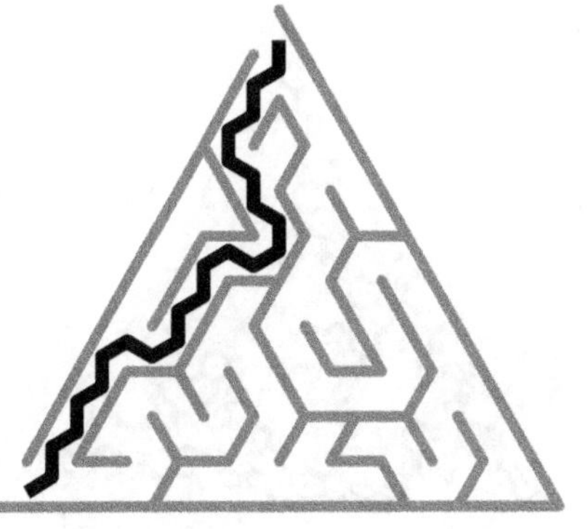

Page 161-1

Page 162-1

Page 163-1

Page 164-1

Page 165-1

Page 166-1

Page 167-1

Page 168-1

Page 169-1

Page 170-1

Page 171-1

Page 172-1

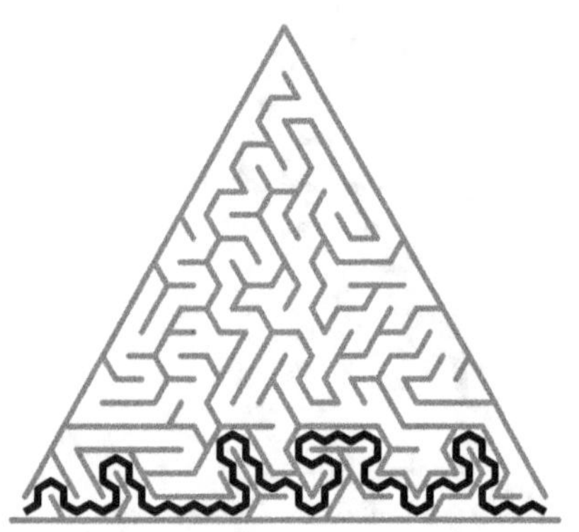

Page 173-1

Page 174-1

Page 175-1

Page 176-1

Page 177-1

Page 178-1

Page 179-1

Page 180-1

Page 181-1

Page 182-1

Page 183-1

Page 184-1

Page 185-1

Page 186-1

Page 187-1

Page 188-1

Page 189-1

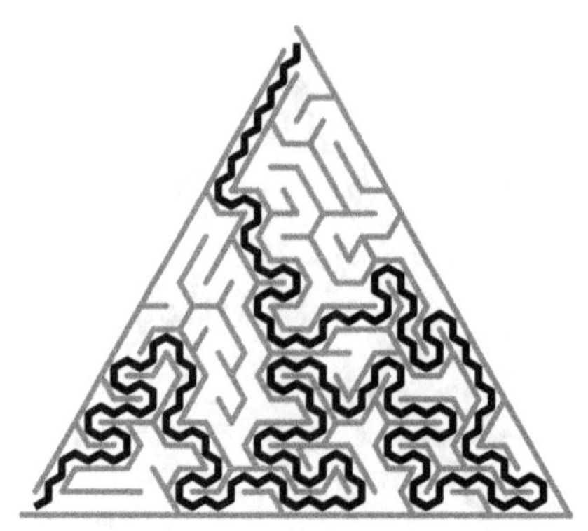

Page 190-1

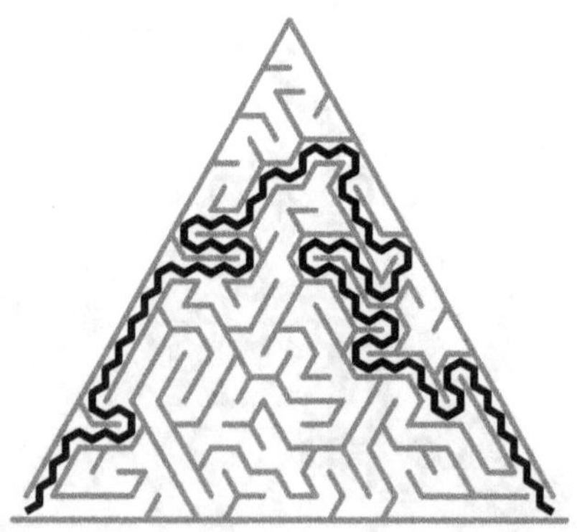

Page 191-1

Page 192-1

Page 193-1

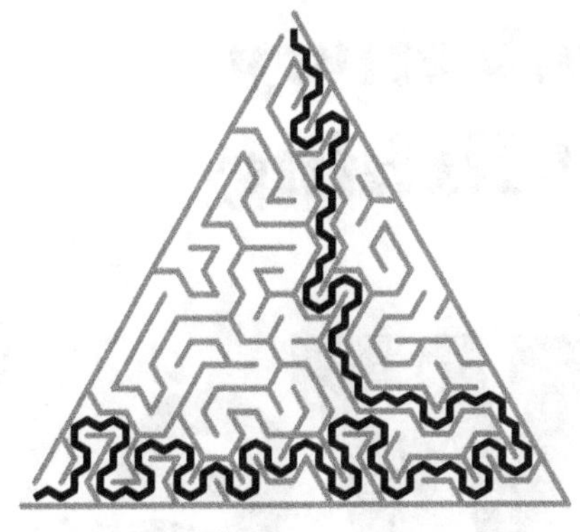

Page 194-1

Page 195-1

Page 196-1

Page 197-1

Page 198-1

Page 199-1

Page 200-1

www.ingramcontent.com/pod-product-compliance
Lightning Source LLC
Chambersburg PA
CBHW080340030726
47595CB00012B/4085